FORGOTTEN NATIONS

FORGOTTEN NATIONS

The Incredible Stories of
Football in the Shadows

CHRIS DEELEY

First published by Pitch Publishing, 2019

Pitch Publishing
A2 Yeoman Gate
Yeoman Way
Worthing
Sussex
BN13 3QZ
www.pitchpublishing.co.uk
info@pitchpublishing.co.uk

ISBN 978 1 78531 456 8

Typesetting and origination by Pitch Publishing

Printed and bound in Great Britain by TJ International Ltd

Contents

Acknowledgements

BLOODY hell. Writing a book is hard. That's good in its own way though because, hey!, I get to freestyle a bit here, on account of having absolutely loads of people to thank for helping me do this.

In no particular order …

Thanks to my mum, who – when I desperately asked for 'some words for the book' before my birthday – diligently spent god only knows how long finding and writing out a sheet of 500 football-related words, conjunctions, nations and other things I could slot into this thing, which feels now like a behemoth but will no doubt end up a slim volume. For that, and so, so many other things, I owe you more than I could ever give back. To my grandma, who helped me summon up the guts to drop out of uni and dive headfirst into what became a career as a writer.

Dad … thank you so, so much for never pushing me to be a Burnley fan. That's possibly the greatest debt of the lot.

Mr Evans, who took a 17-year-old dickhead who took his English A-Level class on a bet and spent a year making him absolutely adore writing (me, the dickhead was me, I was the dickhead, just to be clear). Everyone deserves a teacher so enthusiastic, so giving and so caring for both his subject and his students, and it's a shame that not everyone will have one.

Scott Saunders and Andy Headspeath, friendships forged in Google Hangouts and a tiny little office in Holborn. You're both better than me at FIFA, but I've got you both beat when it comes to taking selfies. Seriously though, this book wouldn't have happened without both of your help and support and I suppose at this point I have to say that I kind of sort of appreciate you, you pricks.

Nick Savage and Matt Barnes, who brought me in and dragged me kicking and screaming up the ladder at 90min before they *took off and abandoned us, the bastards.*

Jack Gallagher for test-reading a couple of draft chapters when I was starting to waver, and Jude Summerfield and Toby Cudworth for keeping me so incredibly down to earth.

Siren. I would be even more of a shambles without you around; it's been too long and I know how much sincerity makes you uncomfortable so I'm not even going to end this on a joke.

The Superhunk Clubhouse. My mates. My pals. You hype me up when I need it and smack me right back down when I buy into it too much. Iggs, Carl, I'm sorry you have to find a new pastime now you can't just shout 'WRITE YOUR BOOK' at me every time I tweet.

The cats. Bread, bames yes is goob, Från, Auj, River. Lottie.

To The Landlord Hater, who managed to predict exactly how and how much I would despise people asking, 'how's the book coming along?' months before it started happening, and basically mapped out my entire mental journey from 'resenting the whole project for existing' through 'resenting myself for thinking it was a good idea' to the final point of 'oh, it's done'.

Acknowledgements

Paul Camillin at Pitch, for his patience for my health and reckless disregard for deadlines. The Guerilla Cricket crew – I'm sorry I haven't been around too much lately. Busy, y'know? Ceri, and Matt, because having people around who've known you forever is very, very good for keeping you grounded, and Charli for letting me ruin a trip to Croatia by thinking about writing instead of having fun.

Everyone who donated their time to be interviewed for this book, thank you – Jack Thorpe especially, just for being the nicest man on the planet.

The NHS, because having a state-sponsored mental breakdown is a hell of a lot better than having to pull through one by yourself.

And Dan Lucas. For always reminding me that being passionate about the things you don't like is fun, but being passionate about the things you love is what lasts. I miss you like fuck, mate. Bugger neutrality.

Preface

FOOTBALL is a stupid thing to write a serious book about. Football is a game (at best a sport, but that's just what we call a game that has some running around in it) where a couple of groups of people try to kick a pumped-up ball into one of two rectangles.

The players aren't allowed to pick up the ball, except the ones who are. The players aren't allowed to touch each other, except they are – but only with a certain physical intensity of impact. Except on the occasions where they hit the ball first, or if the referee doesn't see it.

It's a game of 90 minutes, give or take, ultimately decided by a couple of moments. One piece of brilliance, or one mistake. Hell, football isn't just a stupid thing to write a serious book about, it's just a stupid thing.

But it's a stupid thing that people play everywhere. It's a stupid thing that connects people more than politics, more than language, more than borders. It's a stupid thing that stirs the most intense emotions in the most rational people.

I make my living as a football journalist; I edit at a football website called 90min. In an average day, I'll probably read, write or tweak at least 25 pieces of writing about football, whether they're in 90min or one of the other 17 million publications who publish pieces about the game every day, and the vast majority of them are … absurd.

A business wants to hire the services of a professional – not the best in his field, but probably somewhere around the top 1,000. They're thinking about possibly, maybe, paying another business £10m in compensation to acquire him, before paying him a few million more per year to come and work for them.

The people who like that business, who buy that business's merchandise and use the fact that they like that particular business as one of their main personality traits have very strong opinions about this potential new employee. They may never have seen him perform his services on any consistent basis, and they certainly can't match him for his talent in his own field, but they have strong feelings and by god are they going to let everyone on social media know about them.

Meanwhile, the professional is courting offers from a couple of rival competing businesses. A friend of the person in question tells a newspaper that he's 'conflicted' about where he might go – whether his dog will prefer the climate in Andalusia or in Croydon, whether his wife will prefer the shopping and the social life in one place or the other.

Each of these companies is thinking about hiring the services of a different professional of essentially equal quality at the same time, sending subcontractors to their places of work to see just how well they're doing their job on a specific day. The professional's current company might decide not to let him go at all, not until they have a replacement ready.

Oh, and all of these transactions have to take place within a set time frame or be put off for another six months.

In football, there are probably 20 news articles on that saga, all spread out over the course of a month or so. And it happens for every club, for hundreds of players, all the time, forever. Then there are the writers penning the columns about why the move may or may not be a good idea, the ex-professional players giving their own completely uninformed 'reckons', the 'who is this guy, anyway?' profiles.

Ninety-five per cent of those transfers, the ones writers and editors spend days researching and writing about and editing, and that fans gobble up in their millions, never happen.

Seriously, writing about the processes of football can be profoundly stupid.

That's why *Forgotten Nations* isn't about football. Not really, anyway. Because the least interesting part of football is, very often, the football part. The transfers, the speculation, the constant navel-gazing and overanalysis of a split-second decision.

The thing that makes football such a fascinating subject is the people who play it. Because the game is *so* widespread – played in over 200 countries by hundreds of millions of people – it has some of the world's most fascinating characters. Because it's a competitive endeavour, narratives form. Because it means so much to so many people, the game itself carries an inherent power beyond any other organised activity that humanity as a whole takes part in.

Football is played for fun in gated communities by multimillionaires' heirs. It's played in dusty alleys by children who sleep under tarpaulins by railway tracks. There isn't a single kind of story that football *doesn't* have to tell.

Turns out football isn't a stupid thing to write a serious book about. It's the *greatest* thing to write a serious book about. Around every corner, a story of football being played in the most absurd circumstances. By the most incredible people. By a hell of a lot of bang average people too, you'll find no arguments there, but who cares?

Maybe I'm a romantic, or an idealist (or just a pretentious hipster masquerading as a football fan, as a few people on Twitter might tell you), but I firmly believe that football is at its best when it's as far removed from football as possible. When every kick *means* something, whether that's on a macro level or, better, on a tiny little individual level.

That's why I've made football such a huge part of my life. That's why I've been jumping on last-minute flights to visit amateur teams. Because nothing does stories like football does stories.

So let's tell them.

Introduction

IN a haze of warm north London rain in the summer of 2018, Béla Fejér dived to his right, threw out both his hands and made a save at a football match. In doing so, he won his Karpatalja team the CONIFA World Football Cup – and became a political dissident.

The story of him and his team-mates is an extraordinary one, but one which is echoed – in theme if not in specificities – across the fragmented world of non-FIFA football.

This book is an attempt to tell some of these stories – and in doing so, shed some light on some countries, cultures and peoples who have often fallen between the cracks of the international community.

An early word, then, on that. While this book is called *Forgotten Nations*, very few of the football teams contained within it are from 'proper' countries. There are self-governing states, de facto nations, a smattering of displaced peoples and one bioregion. Questions of borders and arbitrary statehood are unavoidable when looking at places like Abkhazia and Matabeleland, Northern Cyprus and Tibet.

An organisation like CONIFA (The Confederation of Independent Football Associations) has never been more relevant than in the current geopolitical climate. Borders, in previous generations, have shifted and morphed and changed, not quite fluid but certainly capable of morphing from one year to the next. The 21st century – and, really, the end of the post-Cold War reshuffle in eastern Europe – has seen the creation of 'new nations' grind to a more or less complete halt.

The only 'new' nations recognised by the UN since the turn of the millennium have been Timor-Leste, Montenegro (see post-Cold War reshuffle, again) and South Sudan. That isn't to say that there aren't new regions which fulfil the majority of the criteria for statehood – Somaliland and Abkhazia are functionally countries in all but name – but the international community has moved the goalposts and is unlikely to collectively validate a new state in the short to medium term.

Part of that is due to the status quo, real or otherwise, that a continued set of worldwide borders implies. Another part is more self-interested. Put simply, a handful of large countries have overwhelmingly strong influences, and play politics with who they will and will not recognise. Russia will call to recognise a state, a handful of small nations will back that recognition in order to keep relations cordial with Putin and co (and, of course, reap the minor economic benefits implicit in that), while others will oppose the move simply because of Russia's involvement.

When superpowers play politics with the validity of other nations, or potential nations, the whole situation becomes a quagmire which is near impossible to navigate. The path to legitimised statehood has never been more complicated to traverse. That's when people start falling through the cracks.

As tempting as it is to pontificate for chapters and chapters on end about the notion of statehood and the value of borders in an ever more globalised world landscape, this isn't the book for that. Some of the more thoughtful recent writing on those issues can be found in Joshua Keating's *Invisible Countries* and in parts of *Revolting Prostitutes*, co-authored by Juno Mac and Molly Smith. Both offer perspectives on the issues far beyond the scope of this book. After all, we're talking football here. Mostly.

I say 'mostly' because there really is no such thing as 'just football'. Football stripped of its wider context is nothing, a shell of the world's most popular sport. Football stripped of context has no rivalries, no branching narratives – in short, no soul. Would it be simpler if football were alone, a pure, sterile piece of sporting expression? Maybe. Would it be recognisable as the same game, the same experience? Never.

There are those who will claim that sport and politics do not mix. It's important to get to know these people, because it allows you to figure out if they're liars, cowards or merely naive. Politics has always been intertwined with sport, and will always be – and in football more than most. Look, from the very top of the game, at Barcelona, arguably Spain's biggest club, being a driving force in the movement for Catalan independence. Look at the English FA's recent battle with FIFA to allow their players to honour the country's military history by wearing poppies. Look at the way every ruling regime in history has used their nation's sporting prowess as a propaganda arm.

Where there is sport, there are people. Where there are people, there are politics.

CONIFA claim to be an apolitical organisation. While that claim is always delivered with what appears to be complete sincerity, it's difficult not to be sceptical.

What's true is that CONIFA is unlikely to *exclude* any potential member on political grounds. They have a simple (for a given value of simple) list of ten criteria, of which a potential member must meet one or more to qualify. That's it.

1. The Football Association is a member of one of the six continental confederations of FIFA.
2. The entity represented by the Football Association is a member of the IOC.
3. The entity represented by the Football Association is a member of one of the member federations of ARISF.
4. The entity represented by the Football Association is in possession of an ISO 3166-1 country code.
5. The entity represented by the Football Association is a de facto independent territory.
6. The entity represented by the Football Association is included on the United Nations list of non-self-governing territories.
7. The entity represented by the Football Association is included in the directory of countries and territories of the TCC.
8. The entity represented by the Football Association is a member of UNPO and/or FUEN.
9. The entity represented by the Football Association is a minority included in the World Directory of Minorities and Indigenous Peoples.
10. The entity represented by the Football Association is a linguistic minority, the

language of which is included on the ISO
639-2 list.

Beyond that, an oft-repeated mantra by those involved in decision-making at CONIFA goes thusly:

'FIFA tells you who you are. We ask you who you are.'

It's a laudable statement, and one which resonates in the modern era of personal self-identification. It's also, and I feel that this is crucial, not a statement designed at any point to line any individual's pockets. CONIFA's helpers and executive committee are all volunteers. The majority work in day jobs. Their belief in the organisation and its mission – football for all – is untainted by any monetary bonuses.

Acts of political expression by teams are banned while playing in CONIFA events – Xherdan Shaqiri's Kosovo-Albanian eagle hand gesture when playing Serbia at FIFA's World Cup in Russia would have been frowned upon, certainly – and the message is always simple. CONIFA is here to allow people to play football under whatsoever flag they wish. Anything else is irrelevant.

But even with the best will in the world, even with pure hearts and crystal-clear intentions, calling CONIFA apolitical is a farce. The existence of Tibet as a singular entity is one of the most frequently contested issues in the Far East and, whatever your ideals, it's near impossible to insist in good faith that accepting a Tibetan team into your membership, giving them an invite to your showpiece event in London, flying their flag and inviting a cultural display at that event's opening ceremony is not a political act.

Whether we should be in a societal place where existence and self-identification *should* be defined as political acts is another question entirely. But guess what? It's a question that can't be answered without bringing politics into the measure.

None of this is said to denigrate the work done by CONIFA's volunteers, or its aims. Nor, indeed, is it meant as a criticism of its actions. I merely raise this point to demonstrate the tightrope that the organisation and so many of its members walk on a near daily basis, between being just a football team and being a political symbol. For the first time last year, one member Football Association fell off that tightrope, and how CONIFA deal with that may be the defining moment in its history thus far.

But we'll get to that later.

* * * *

Large parts of this book will be taken from London in the summer of 2018, in that fortnight between the end of the Premier League season and the start of the FIFA World Cup in Russia, when football grounds around the capital were filled with flags they'd never seen before. When the eyes of the world turned to watch 16 teams play in CONIFA's most expansive World Football Cup to date.

I spent almost every waking hour of the tournament – and the days before and after – either at stadiums, at the tournament base in north London or taking buses and overground trains to parts of the city I wasn't sure existed outside of tube map trivia quizzes.

The tournament lasted a scant ten days from start to finish, packing in a frankly ridiculous 41 matches, 158 goals from 90 scorers (92 with own goals) and – it is tournament football after all – five penalty shoot-outs. The football was fast and often furious. All that the teams represented beyond the game itself somehow meant that the football mattered most of all. That meaning, that symbolism, was all distilled into 90 minutes, 22 men and change, and a ball.

The quality was varied – although there weren't many of the colossal mismatches that some casual observers had feared coming into the tournament – but that one thing that fans demand was undeniable. The passion. Sorry London readers, the *pashhhhunnnnn*. Tackles were full-blooded; every game *meant* something.

And then … it stopped. Teams flew home and went back to their day jobs. International footballers became office workers and builders, waiting for their next chance to show themselves on a world stage again.

That's where the tournament ended, and that's where the work really started.

* * * *

CONIFA itself is a volunteer-run organisation, rising out of the ashes of the Nouvelle Fédération-Board, which more or less ran non-FIFA football, organising its own 'World Cup' events – the first of which was won by Sapmi, a team representing the Sami people around the north of the general Nordic area.

The score, for the record, was 21-1. For those reading this for the human aspect rather than the footballing one, I'll let you in on a secret: that's an absolute hiding. That's a spanking of near-historic proportions, and one that tends to come of a match or tournament where the organisation is a little … free-form.

The Nouvelle Fédération-Board ceased operations in 2013, at which point CONIFA sprung up. Headed up by president Per-Anders Blind, a Sami reindeer herder (a small herd, he says, of only around 10,000), CONIFA is comprised of 51 member associations at time of writing, covering five continents. South America's absence is something of a surprise given the area's notorious love of football and various indigenous peoples, while Antarctica ... well, that's more straightforward. Have you tried playing football in snowshoes? Graceful it ain't.

Blind was joined in his CONIFA venture by a German named Sascha Düerkop, who ... well, I've put a lot of thought into describing Sascha over the course of writing this book. To call him a lunatic would be reductive, and more than a little offensive. To call him a football obsessive would fail to convey the devotion he has to the sport. To call him a six-foot-something mass of near-terrifying Teutonic intensity wrapped in jeans and a football shirt would be ... well, it'd be accurate, but not very helpful.

A sentence isn't enough. It just isn't. Düerkop came to CONIFA by chance, asked by a team representing the Cascadia region of North America if he could attend a Nouvelle Fédération-Board on their behalf, the meeting being near him in Munich and North America being, notably, not. How did he know that team? He'd run out of FIFA national team shirts to collect – over 200 and counting – and was starting to dive into the world of non-FIFA to get his fix.

His chance presence at the NF-Board meeting turned out to be, with little exaggeration, one of the most important moments in the recent history of non-FIFA football – because at that meeting, the organisation collapsed. Entirely. A mass of infighting saw the organisation more or less implode on the spot and, as the only person to collect a full set of names and contact details, Düerkop became the point of contact for former NF-Board referee Blind when the serious-faced Sami decided to pick up the pieces. He was installed as General Secretary from day one.

Within a year, CONIFA was hosting its first World Football Cup in Östersund, Sweden. The County of Nice team won, came second in the European Football Cup the following year and promptly disappeared from the next three continental and world tournaments. That kind of thing happens a lot in CONIFA.

* * * *

This book isn't a CONIFA encyclopaedia. There aren't enough pages, there are too many teams who are just balls-out impossible to get in contact with, and I'd have got bored about halfway through writing it. This is a book of stories – of people, of places, of teams, of histories. Football is never as interesting as the people playing it, and rarely as interesting as the places it's being played.

It was one person's story that got me interested in CONIFA in the first place. Sitting in a shared office building in a little side room with two other editors at 90min, the football website I've worked at for over five years, we got looking at some pretty funky football shirts.

One of my colleagues, Andy Headspeath, got off his backside and did some digging around on where these shirts – all for African teams, all utterly unique, all gaudy and brilliant – were coming from, and found that they were the work of AMS Clothing. AMS Clothing, in turn, was Luke Westcott, a 23-year-old student in Australia who just so happened to design football shirts for fun.

That fun became a little business, and ended in Westcott becoming a kit supplier to a number of teams. South Sudan wore an AMS kit in their first Africa Cup of Nations qualifier,

Sierra Leone became an AMS team, as did Djibouti. Westcott travelled to South Sudan for their first game in 'his' kit and met FIFA president Gianni Infantino, who now has a Sudanese shirt to add to what might, theoretically, be a pretty nice collection.

Andy ended up interviewing Westcott for another football website, The Set Pieces, and getting sent a couple of shirts in the bargain – including that of Eritrea, FIFA's lowest ranked team, and Barawa.

Full disclosure: I had absolutely no idea who Barawa were at that point. A club? A place? It certainly wasn't a country I was aware of – but the kit, with its flashy design and sponsored by Red Sea Exotic Fish (find me a better sponsor of a football team, seriously), hung on our office wall proudly.

Without Westcott (and to be fair, without Andy doing the legwork to find him, dig into Barawa and set me off down the CONIFA rabbit hole), this book would never have happened. I'd have sat blissfully ignorant as some of the most incredible characters carried on doing their thing in the shadows. I might've paid attention when the World Football Cup came to London (I am an inveterate football hipster, of course), but it would've been a curiosity rather than a near obsession.

Since they aren't going to get a full chapter of their own, Barawa should probably get a nod here.

Representing the Somali diaspora in England and worldwide, the Barawa FA takes its name from a port town in the south-west of Somalia and has strong ties with the Bravanese community back in their home country – aiming to use football to keep cultural ties strong, and help those back in the conflict-stricken country.

Terror group Al-Shabaab have been particularly active in Somalia, and especially in Barawa – where they banned sporting activity before being driven out by African Union and Somali armed forces in recent years. When an Al-Shabaab bomb killed five and injured a number of others in an attack in Barawa in 2018, it wasn't a coincidence that the explosive was planted at the town's football stadium.

Al-Shabaab, by the way? Literally translates to 'The Lads'. There's something incredibly 21st century about that, isn't there? It'd be a very different world if Ireland (or, at least, Britain's actions in Ireland or, failing that, a more complicated set of events that are far too sensitive for a glib throwaway line) had produced Na Buachaillí rather than the IRA, or if Spain had been terrorised by the Basque Mutilak.

As they represent the diaspora rather than the local Bravanese population, the Barawa FA are located in London – and were the official hosts for the 2018 CONIFA World Football Cup. It was somewhat easier to sell than taking everyone over to southern Somalia, although the 2020 edition is set to be held in Somaliland, a self-declared independent state of around four million people which is trying to break away from Somalia as a whole.

Barawa's first competitive game inside CONIFA, putting aside some friendlies played in the two years since their 2016 admission to the organisation, was their 2018 World Football Cup opener in Bromley.

For the first time in some time, the eyes of the world's media – seriously, there were Sky cameras and all – were on Barawa. For a positive story. Alright, and a little bit because Mark Clattenburg, a 'celebrity' referee who has taken charge of Champions League, FA Cup, European Championship and Olympic finals, was officiating the game.

Despite failing to win their last three games in the lead up to the tournament, Barawa turned it on under the lights at

Bromley's Hayes Lane, taking the lead early against outsiders Tamil Eelam and pushing home their advantage brilliantly to secure a 4-0 win. A goal-of-the-tournament contender from Hendon FC midfielder Shaun Lucien was the pick of the strikes, as hardcore and casual fans mingled on the sidelines.

The late addition of striker Mohamed Bettamer wasn't enough to push Barawa past Cascadia in their second group game, going down 2-1 to the North American side, but a controversial 2-0 win over Ellan Vannin the following day secured the hosts' passage through to the quarter-finals. Off-field commitments and unexpected availabilities meant that the team's first knockout game was a massive anticlimax though, Northern Cyprus kicking the seven hells out of a significantly weakened side to win 8-0.

The two placement games which followed ended up more or less along the same lines: Panjab – another largely UK-based side – racking up five goals without reply before Western Armenia finished the tournament with a 7-0 thrashing of the hosts in Haringey.

That's the overview. When it comes to subplots ... well. One of the teams they played was the subject of a protest letter from a high commissioner, another met as a squad for the first time 24 hours before the start of the tournament and a third could have got the whole competition cancelled. One Barawa game led to the first ever expulsion of a team from CONIFA's ranks, and the last two sides they played *absolutely hate each other*.

Welcome to non-FIFA football.

Welcome to the home of the *Forgotten Nations*.

Cascadia – America, But Not

HE Hive, Barnet FC's ground and training complex, is a sparkling example of the things that lower league clubs can do with the right investment and smart planning. Arriving there the day before the 2018 World Football Cup kicks off, there are some LA Galaxy II gazebos set up beside the 3G pitches, with watchful coaches and scouts looking for the next big thing at their trial session.

In another timeline, one or two of the Cascadia team might be strutting their stuff on those artificial pitches, looking to earn a move to a club in the States. In this one though, Cascadia find themselves shunted to the very edge of Barnet's complex – a few hundred yards from the slick stadium and high-tech pitches, on a pitch that wouldn't have looked out of place in an amateur Sunday League ground. Whose groundsman had died.

Jack Thorpe is the only man there – a Wolves scout who, in his spare time, has helped Cascadia coaches James Nichols, Shaun Gardner and Stuart Dixon put together a band of 20ish players to compete in London.

He isn't happy.

'I think there have been some foxes on the pitch or something,' he says by way of greeting. 'There are holes just fucking ... everywhere.'

There are. There's a minor crater inside the centre circle – at least the pitch has been marked out (small mercies) – and a few smaller troughs scattered around, but the showstopper is about five yards outside one of the penalty boxes: a hole almost perfectly the size of a grown man's foot, which would swallow him to mid-shin.

It's an inauspicious start to Cascadia's first ever training session as a football team; a couple of coaches and 23 (actually 22 – one got lost in transit) strangers traipsing over to the outskirts of Barnet's training ground.

With the second-rate pitch and mismatched kits, it's hard not to feel a sense that these are the players the US has already rejected, just a few hundred yards away from trials for one of Major League Soccer's biggest teams.

That sense dissipates quickly upon talking to the players – partly because most of them seem too young to have been rejected by anyone but a school classmate yet, but primarily because the majority of them speak with London accents.

Not solely because of CONIFA's *sliiiiightly* loose criteria for player qualification, either.

Allow me ...

* * * *

The region referred to as Cascadia is pretty massive, consisting of (deep breath now) all of the state of Washington, most of Oregon, Idaho and British Columbia, some of northern California, and little bits of Montana, Wyoming, Nevada, Alaska and Yukon.

It's not just a region, you see, it's a bioregion. Now, a glimpse behind the curtain: my original notes on this chapter read, at this point, 'Explain where Cascadia is. It's a "bioregion" full of hippies in North America. Now explain what a bioregion is, dummy'.

So now I, the dummy, will explain what a bioregion is in fairly short words – not because I don't trust your intelligence but because I don't trust my own.

One way to look at the idea of a bioregion is to consider a map as if the boundaries were drawn by nature, rather than being man-made and relatively arbitrary. It's an ecological, environmental region rather than one defined by population or political lines. It's a recognised concept – the World Wildlife Fund classifies it as 'larger than an ecoregion but smaller than an ecozone', which I'll grant is a spectacularly useless definition if you don't know what those are either, but the point is that … it's a thing, okay? It's a thing. Of course, people don't usually adopt them as pseudo-states.

The defining feature of Cascadia specifically is (surprise!) the Cascade mountain range, which runs as a spine down what is generally considered Cascadian 'territory'. Full of coniferous tree forests, bears (some), coyotes (more), deer, elk, moose (more again), cougars (thousands) and wolves (fewer), Cascadia is a diverse ecological region. Apparently. I'm not an expert, but people who are seem to agree on that point, so who am I to argue?

There are some volcanos there too, it being a mountain range and all that, although all but one are dormant. That one is Mount St Helens, which erupted in 1980. That eruption was the deadliest in United States history – if you're going, go big – and some more minor activity has been observed there in the decades since. I sat through a lot of geography lessons about Mount St Helens in a comp in south Wales maybe 15 years ago. Did not expect it to ever come up again in my life. A surprise around every corner in adult life, eh?

Anyway, that's Cascadia's boundaries and the briefest primer on bioregions, but what about the people who live there? More to the point, what about the people who live there *and* identify as Cascadian?

Given the traditionally left-wing political leanings of the north-west of the United States and British Columbia, it's not a surprise that a lot of self-identifying Cascadians are both politically active and left-leaning, usually uniting under the unofficial flag of the region: the Doug.

Named for the tree which features in its centre, the Douglas fir, the Doug flag's background is three horizontal stripes, blue over white over green. Designed by student Alexander Baretich in the 90s, the flag quickly earned near-ubiquitous status at protests and political rallies across Cascadia, particularly in Seattle and Portland.

Explaining his vision for the flag some years later – and indeed his vision for the region itself – Baretich said, 'The flag conveys something far more tangible than an abstract concept of demarcation of space; the flag captures that love of living communities in our bioregion. Unlike many flags, this is not a flag of blood, nor of the glory of a nation, but a love of the bioregion, our ecological family and its natural boundaries, the place in which we live and love.'

Like I said. Full of hippies.

But hippies with a point. In a continent doing its level best to ignore the encroaching threat of climate change, environmental awareness is *important as hell*. It's no coincidence that the flag also shows up at a number of the region's gay pride parades and Occupy demonstrations; it's become a symbol for people in the area who want to bring through important issues on the back of … well, caring about the place they live, and the people who live there.

There are some looming threats to those ideals though. A number of white nationalists have piggybacked on the idea of a separatist, nationalist Cascadia. The region is already overwhelmingly white in its population, and the idea of a separated, ecologically classical 'utopia' has resonated with some people who many Cascadians would rather stay a long, long way away from.

One student arrested in Oregon for hate crimes in recent years had both a Confederate flag and a Cascadian one hanging in his room. White nationalist Jeremy Christian, who killed two people on a train in Portland in 2017 after shouting racist slurs at a pair of teenage girls, had called for 'Cascadia as a white homeland' on his Facebook page before the killings. It's clear that these people don't represent Cascadia or Cascadian ideology as a whole, but to ignore the existence of the movement would appear to be dangerously ignorant. What'll happen? Who knows? Predicting American political developments is like trying to guess which precious vase a drunk toddler might smash if you put them in a room full of them.

On to less delicate matters. Cascadia has three Major League Soccer teams: the Portland Timbers (whose fan group have adopted the Doug flag), the Seattle Sounders and the Vancouver Whitecaps. The trio played together in the United Soccer League at the start of this century, leading to fans creating the Cascadia Cup, a trophy awarded to the team with the best results in a mini-league between the trio in their league fixtures against each other at the end of each season.

Seattle's entry to MLS in 2009 meant that they couldn't play for the cup for a couple of seasons, before Portland and Vancouver joined them at the top table in 2011. The competition has been remarkably evenly split since then, with three wins apiece for Vancouver and Seattle and two for Portland, and the matches are some of the most fiercely competitive in the competition. The rivalry is real, and if there's an area which has a claim to be the real homeland for fan culture in North America, it's Cascadia.

* * * *

Wolves scout Jack Thorpe has been the man on the ground in the months leading up to the tournament, scouring the lower leagues for promising players with Cascadian roots who would be willing to give up two weeks of their summer to play for nothing, for a team they've never heard of, with people they've never met.

Jack ended up bringing in more than half of the team, finding players who could be both eligible for the team and good enough to complement the handful of players who were coming over from the US.

'I heard from Paul Watson [Tournament Director of the 2018 competition] that Cascadia were struggling to get a team together,' he told me, 'so I thought it might be fun to help out. I started going through lists of non-league players off the top of my head who I was aware were vaguely American or Canadian and finding contact details for them to make the sales pitch.

'I did my best to make sure there were scouts from professional clubs at their games so that the players had a chance to put themselves in the shop window, which was a big part of the pitch to them.

'Patrick Wilson: I wasn't aware of him as a player but his Football Manager profile said he was Canadian. He thought it was a bit weird that I'd found him "on a game", but he joined up and then asked "hey, do you mind if my brother plays?" Turned out his brother is a pro in Denmark, which was a massive bonus. His brother (Jordan) vice-captained the team!'

For some players, the tournament does the job. Some summer fitness, a chance to get in front of some scouts. Not for all of them though.

'One player, Anthony Wright, I know he'd been a pro at Forest so I knew he must've been half decent but I couldn't find any contract information for him anywhere. I went to one of Banbury's last games of the season to see him play, and I waited outside the ground for him to leave.

'He was really down on football because he'd been taken off in that game, said he was going to go back to America and give up football but I convinced him to play … I don't think he's played a single game of football since. He's gone to uni, and I don't even think he's playing for his uni team. This was his last hurrah.'

The squad is augmented by a handful of actual Americans, led by former MLS star James Riley. The ex-Seattle Sounder had a storied career in the top tier of American domestic football, winning the US Open Cup five times, the MLS Cup once and, earlier in his career, helping New England Revolution to three Eastern Conference titles in as many years.

At the age of 35 and two years into his retirement, his announcement as Cascadia's captain came as something of a surprise – dragged into the setup late on by a journalist who knew him from his playing days.

Riley himself is a native of Seattle now, in many ways the heartland of Cascadia. Diminutive and softly spoken, he represents the opposite of what you might expect an American captain to look like, but he's as fiercely competitive as any American hero of years gone by.

Looking back at Riley's influence in the tournament, one member of the squad explained, 'He had a lot of respect, he's been there and done it, and he commanded that respect really well. Everybody was there to win, but he was *there* to *win*. It was surprising, he'd been retired for two years, but his competitive nature and the way he conducted himself was amazing.

'After our first game he brought everyone into the lobby and was like "right, now we're all going to go to the shops and get two bottles of Lucozade, two bottles of water, protein bars and all that", and it set a real example to the team that if you want to be a footballer, this is the way you need to be.'

There's only so much a captain can do though, no matter how respected they are, and the Cascadia team have known each other for a full 22 hours by the time the first match of the tournament rolls around. It isn't enough for some, with at least one audible whisper of 'sorry, what's your name again?' in the tunnel as the Americans come out to face Ellan Vannin – the team from the Isle of Man.

It takes just 15 minutes for Stephen Whitley to put the Manxmen in the lead, a rasping shot from the edge of the area flying into the roof of the net of teenage goalkeeper Will Marment. Nerves start to jangle among the Cascadia fans in the stands, knowing that this could easily become a drubbing, especially if that barely set glue holding the team together comes unstuck.

If the opener came quickly, the equaliser is like lightning. A long ball over the top releases Calum Ferguson down the left, and the Scottish-born Canada Under-20 international holds off a defender to square the ball to Josh Doughty, who makes no mistake. It's 1-1, and the celebrations are as joyous as they are slightly confused.

Cascadia dominate the rest of the first half, but a blown marking assignment lets Ellan Vannin go into the changing room one goal up at the break. In the second half, the collapse finally materialises and the Americans finish on the end of a 4-1 beating, with captain Riley coming off with a combination of a muscle niggle and a lack of match fitness early in the second period.

On the pitch at full time, Riley tells me, 'They've been together for a while and they're the favourites here, but I thought we did well and had a chance to get a result. To lead out the first Cascadian team here is immense, it brings back memories of being in Seattle with the Sounders's inaugural game – how special it was for the Pacific Northwest, and for American soccer as a whole.

'I thought we were the better team in the first half, but the Isle of Man punished us for some mistakes in the first half. Disappointed to not get the result, but there are a lot of positives to take from our first game given that we met yesterday. For me the calf and the hamstring, plus old age – I told the coach to be aware of it. I pushed through in the first half, but I wanted to be able to push through for the double-header at the weekend.

'We have the players to make it into the winners' bracket; we're just trying to figure out who our best team is. It's almost a trial at the moment, and by the end of the weekend we should have our best team taking shape.'

It takes just two days for him to be proved absolutely right, and heads are turned when goals from Hector Morales and, again, Doughty turn a 1-0 deficit against hosts Barawa into a 2-1 win, a match holding a significance to the tournament which wouldn't become publicly obvious until after the next round of games, leading to Ellan Vannin's eventual banishment from CONIFA.

With scouts from clubs around the UK keeping a close watch on proceedings at the World Football Cup, Doughty's good performances in back-to-back games have caught the eye, not for the first time.

As a 17-year-old, the Canadian moved from Real Salt Lake to Manchester United, drawing comparisons to Dimitar Berbatov from his Canada Under-20 manager. Delays with international clearance followed though, and the move dragged on. He arrived highly rated, despite the delay, and was clearly confident in his chances of breaking through at the highest level.

After his medical in 2014, he told an American website, 'I will be playing mainly with the United Under-21s; however, I might play with the Under-18s to get back up to speed. I can play for Canada, England and hopefully will be eligible for the US soon [but] I am still undecided on which team I will play for at the moment.'

United are a club famous for bringing through youth players into their first team but, unlike players like Timothy Fosu-Mensah, Andreas Pereira and Axel Tuanzebe, who are roughly the same age as the young Canadian, Doughty didn't break into the first team.

In fact, he barely featured for the Under-21s, where he had previously been so confident of making a mark. While Marcus Rashford, his United youth team-mate, broke into the first team to score four goals in his first two senior games, Doughty floundered. Quietly, over the winter of 2016, he left the club and returned to the US. Homesickness was given as a reason for his failure to adapt to life at United's Carrington training complex, and he more or less fell out of the game on a recognisable level until he popped up in Cascadia's squad.

In a Cascadia squad who bonded together almost instantly under James Riley's captaincy, Doughty stuck out like a sore thumb, clearly on the outside of the group, seemingly reluctant to engage with his team-mates. Whether it was a symptom of being burned by his time at United or a possible reason for his apparent failure to integrate away from home, it was obvious – and hard to determine the root cause of, because he wasn't keen on talking to me, either.

It didn't go unnoticed, one team-mate admitting after the tournament that he would never have guessed Doughty had been a highly touted prospect at one of the world's biggest clubs, and another questioning whether he took his time with Cascadia seriously.

He started the tournament well, though, scoring in each of the first two games and being offered a trial at Middlesbrough, playing in the second tier of English football. That trial might not have come if the scout hadn't left before full time, when Doughty was sent off for sparking off a melee by, as they might say in Wales, 'starting on' one of the Barawa players.

It didn't really matter though; he didn't take the trial, and went back to North America. The takeaway was pretty clear. He was a talented player – you don't stay at Manchester United for as long as he did without that – but there was something else going on under the surface.

Sunday dawns and, just 24 hours after breathing life into their World Football Cup campaign, Cascadia face a do or die scenario. Again. Tamil Eelam have been the group's whipping boys so far, but Nichols and co come into the match knowing that just a win won't necessarily be enough, with their goal difference sitting at -2 after their opening game drubbing.

Sure enough, Barawa lead Ellan Vannin at half-time thanks to a strike from controversial striker Mohamed Bettamer, leaving the Americans with a mountain to climb. Goals from Tayshan Hayden-Smith and Jon Nouble – brother of former Chelsea and West Ham product Frank – mean that each of the three competing teams are sat on a provisional six points, but Cascadia are four goals off a qualification spot.

Barawa score one just after half-time to make the task a shade more manageable, but a stubborn Tamil team have kept the North Americans to just two more goals in the second half. With less than five minutes to go, Cascadia are set to be the only team to go out with two wins – until target man Nouble, an absolute unit, a 6ft 4in Gulliver towering above his team of Lilliputians, cuts in from the left flank and bends a brilliant, dipping shot around the Tamil goalkeeper from the edge of the area. It's like a mountain growing an arm and painting the Mona Lisa, like a volcano retraining as a nail technician. A force of nature can be beautiful, sure, but on an epic scale. This is precision, finesse, and detail. Cascadia, though they don't know it yet, are through.

All teams are granted a rest day between the group stage and the start of the knockout rounds. A good thing too, because three games in four days, especially when you have to push right to the finish line of your final match, is an absolutely knackering proposition. When your captain hasn't played in two years and is starting to creak a little, it becomes even more important.

There seems to be something about Sutton's Gander Green Lane though, the scene of that humbling opening day loss to Ellan Vannin. It's a warm Tuesday evening when Cascadia return to the scene of their first ever match to face Karpatalja, and the first half of the match … well, the first half of the match isn't really worth spending much time on. Karpatalja probe and prod at the Cascadian side, who defend stoutly and break with pace. Nobody scores. Half-time arrives.

When the second half starts, Karpatalja get a massive slice of luck – a speculative shot from 25 yards out hit straight at goalkeeper Will Marment, who completely fails to gather it, parrying it straight back out into the middle of the box. Gergő Gyürki pounces, putting away the simplest finish in the world, and Cascadia are behind.

The second goal is a shambles of defending, one which Nichols is still fuming about at full time. Karpataljan defender Robert Molnar picks up the ball right out on the wing, just inside the Cascadia half. A quick shimmy takes him around Cascadia vice-captain Jordan Wilson, before two more men in blue, white and green shirts completely whiff on attempted tackles.

Patrick Wilson, Jordan's brother, is turned absolutely inside out in the penalty area before Molnar's eventual shot is *finally* blocked.

The rebound falls to Ronald Takács. He taps past a stranded Marment in goal to double the lead. Sometimes football isn't fair.

It's the second goal that finally wakes Cascadia up as dusk begins to set across south London, the pitch bathed in an orangey late-evening glow as North America's only representatives finally perk up and start to attack with vigour. Winger Max Oldham, later named player of the tournament by at least one publication, is at the heart of a number of the attacks. Driving forward powerfully, he creates a couple of half (really, quarter) chances before going through the middle of two Karpatalja defenders to set up Hamza Haddadi. He scores. With just ten minutes remaining, Cascadia are back in the game … somehow.

It isn't enough. An absolutely monstrous kick from Karpatalja goalkeeper Béla Fejér takes out the whole Cascadia team, bouncing once on the edge of the penalty area and hanging high in the air as Zsolt Gajdos and Cascadia's Joey Censoni battle to win the header when it comes down again. Censoni pushes Gajdos in the back, the referee gives a penalty, and Gajdos (**FOOTBALL CLICHÉ ALERT**) dusts himself off to take the penalty and seal Karpatalja's progress to the semi-finals.

The dream is over. Exactly a week after the squad met for the first time, they've been knocked out of the competition they were assembled to win. It was, ultimately, a step too far.

* * * *

When I spoke to Oldham a little after the competition was wrapped up, he admitted, 'I think the idea of the tournament was really good, but it was a really hard job for the manager to pick a team because he didn't know everything about everybody. The scheduling though … it was impossible. We played three games in four days, then we had the quarter-final after that. I think I played 90 minutes in every game and I was just knackered by the time the quarter-final came.

'The guys from Karpatalja, they'd all played together multiple times beforehand, and had a much deeper bench. Their continuity and the fact that they could rely on people off the bench was a big part of the reason they were fresher and that they won that match. Add that into the fact that we'd just played three games in four days and that was that. They had some good players on their team though.'

It became clear just how good those Karpatalja players were a few days later when they eased through their semi-final against Székely Land, then beat Northern Cyprus on penalties to become CONIFA world champions.

As for Cascadia, their final two games – in the placement round, much to the chagrin of the coaches and players – provided a chance to hit back and prove themselves against the other beaten quarter-finalists. They took that opportunity with both hands against Western Armenia in the first of their two placement games, absolutely racing out of the blocks to shut down the Armenians and secure a 4-0 win, Calum Ferguson striking twice while Oldham finally got the goal his consistent performances had deserved.

The Corinthian-Casuals winger was one of a number of British-based players in the Cascadia team in London, fresh off an excellent season for Britain's highest ranked fully amateur team. Now living in the capital, Oldham was born in northern California and grew up there, although he admits that he always considered himself an England fan through his father.

Oldham was one of a number of players in the Cascadia side playing while being acutely aware of the scouts from lower league clubs who came to London for a week to find some rough diamonds who could be cut and shined into full-time professionals. For him, 24 at the time of the tournament, it came at the perfect time of his career – nearing his prime, and standing out in a team who appealed to British clubs thanks to the number of players who already live in the country.

His performances earned him a three-week trial with Swindon Town, who were preparing for a season in England's League Two (the fourth tier of the English football pyramid, in that obvious and intuitive way that English football functions). That trial ended without a contract being offered and, despite some interest from clubs in the National League (fifth tier – again, yes, intuitive), Oldham ended up back at Corinthian-Casuals for the following season.

'It feels weird to say it,' he hedged, 'but I was aware that there was some buzz around my name coming into the tournament. The coaches and James actually came up to me before a few games to say "oh, such and such was here to see you play, or this person was here to watch you". Unfortunately none of it worked out, but the tournament certainly benefitted me in that way and I had some great experiences nonetheless.'

Oldham was one of six Cascadia players who featured in every one of the team's matches over the course of the ten-day tournament, but the fatigue implicit in that schedule didn't seem to manifest. Slow out of the blocks, they allowed a skilful Panjab team to race into a 3-0 lead before nicking one goal back as the managers' minds turned to their half-time team talks.

Calum Ferguson scored another brace within 15 minutes of the restart and Cascadia looked for all the world as though they would roar back to win the game inside 90 minutes and complete an incredible turnaround to secure fifth place in the tournament. Panjab stuck to their task, however, forcing a penalty shoot-out in which the first four penalties were missed. The next seven all hit the back of the net, though, before Keaton Levock faltered to blacken Cascadian moods.

Ferguson ended the tournament as Cascadia's highest scorer by some distance, hitting the back of the net five times while none of the other Americans did so more than twice, but was forced to take a break from football after the summer when an ongoing back problem worsened, forcing him to crowdfund surgery in order to give himself a chance of returning to the pitch.

Injury would be a cruel way to cut short a promising career, the Scottish-Canadian forward starting his career at Inverness Caledonian Thistle (of 'Super Caley Go Ballistic, Celtic Are Atrocious' headline fame) and impressing enough to pick up a number of caps for Canada's Under-18 and Under-20 sides.

He bounced around the Scottish leagues for a couple of seasons before the injury which was inhibiting him became too much at the start of the 2018/19 season but, having only turned 24 in early 2019, he has time to bounce back and forge a career in professional football, if his body allows it.

Most teams across the tournament piled into their buses and made their way to Enfield to watch the final and pick up their medals, but the Cascadian delegation who climbed the steps to the roof of the Queen Elizabeth II Stadium for their trophy (oh yeah, every team got a trophy) consisted of just the coach and FA president.

Their reaction summed up the Cascadian approach to the tournament, and laid out exactly why they'll be such a threat at Somaliland 2020, if they go. A muttered 'I don't want a trophy if I haven't won', a brief lift of the pot for the crowd below, and on to the planning stage for the next tournament, and for the future of the team.

Reflecting on the experience a few months later, Oldham agreed with the mindset. 'If you looked on paper,' he said, 'talent-wise we should've gone a lot further. Some people were just there for the experience, but people like myself and a lot of the others, we really wanted to win. James was right, if we're going to pick something up that isn't for winning, what's the point?'

Ellan Vannin –
the Outlaws

I SWEAR, I was never going to write about Ellan Vannin in this book. An Ellan Vannin chapter would have said 'it's the team from the Isle of Man', and then ended really abruptly.

And then they threw an almighty shitfit at the 2018 World Football Cup and became the first team to be expelled from CONIFA. And *that* was, finally, interesting.

Are you ready? Deep breath … okay. Ellan Vannin is not the official Isle of Man football team – that's the Isle of Man Representative County football team, who are essentially a county team affiliated to the English FA. Ellan Vannin, conversely, are an international team set up by the Manx International Football Alliance – an organisation created for that very purpose – in 2013 to give the island a face on the international stage.

Life as an international team started in front of 1,100 people at The Bowl in the Manx capital of Douglas, and went about as well as any international debut ever has (note: this has not been fact-checked at all; there is no list of every team's international debut and I am absolutely too idle to create and populate one), with a 10-0 win over Monaco.

Again, that's the Monaco national team, not the league side. The league side, who play in the top division of French football, would've battered Ellan Vannin and had them with whatever the super-rich eat instead of chips. Possibly fried oyster slices?

While Monaco went away to pay some people to lick their wounds for them, Ellan Vannin earned themselves an invite to the inaugural CONIFA World Football Cup just a few months later in Sapmi – a large cultural region in northern Europe commonly (and slightly incorrectly) called Lapland.

The tournament didn't start perfectly for the Manx side, going 2-0 down in Östersund to 2019 CONIFA European Football Championship hosts Artsakh within half an hour thanks to a brace from Mihran Manasyan, a 25-year-old striker for Alashkert in the Armenian top flight.

However, a dramatic late comeback saw Ellan Vannin hit two goals in the last two minutes – including an injury-time winner from captain Frank Jones – to triumph 3-2 and move to within a whisker of qualification from the three-team group into the quarter-finals.

A hat-trick from Manx striker Calum Morrissey in a 4-2 win over the County of Nice put Ellan Vannin into a quarter-final against Iraqi Kurdistan, which they won on penalties after former (and future) Derry City defender Seamus Sharkey pulled them back from a goal down in the last ten minutes. A 4-1 spanking of Arameans Suryoye followed in the semi-final – although not before Ellan Vannin went 1-0 down early on once again – to set up a final two days later against their one-time groupmates County of Nice.

The two teams went head to head for the second time in the tournament at Östersunds FK's 9,000 capacity Jämtkraft Arena and, after sharing six goals in their group clash, proceeded to play out a blindingly dull 0-0 draw – with County of Nice getting their revenge for the group stage battering, becoming CONIFA's first ever world champions after winning the penalty shoot-out 5-3.

Not content with ruining Ellan Vannin's World Football Cup campaign, County of Nice went on to beat them in the semi-finals of the following summer's European Football Championship in Székely Land – this time triumphing 3-1 inside 90 minutes.

Since that semi-final appearance in 2015, though, the Ellan Vannin team have fallen on harder times. Absent from the 2016 World Football Cup in Abkhazia on the basis of advice from the Home Office, they didn't make it out of their group at the 2017 Euros – finishing sixth after losing a play-off, again on penalties, to Karpatalja.

The Isle of Man Premier League has more or less been taken over by St Georges AFC since they won their first title of the 21st century in 2004, the Douglas-based team winning 13 out of the last 15 top-flight championships. Between them and Corinthians, the Ellan Vannin team is close to a two-club side in its make-up, providing ten and eight players respectively for London 2018.

Then came London 2018. The big one. Not only Ellan Vannin's return to the World Football Cup after missing the 2016 tournament, but the closest they were ever likely to be to a CONIFA tournament geographically, having had to pull out of hosting the 2015 Euros late on in the process.

They arrived in the English capital as the pre-tournament favourites with bookmakers Paddy Power, who were sponsoring the tournament. They won their opening two games by an aggregate score of 6-1. Even as the Manx side kicked off their third and final group match, reigning champions Abkhazia were in the process of failing to qualify from their own group.

And then Ellan Vannin were kicked out of CONIFA.

Rewind a couple of days, back to the second round of Group A matches – in which Ellan Vannin cruised past Tamil Eelam 2-0 and Cascadia recovered from an opening day defeat to beat nominal hosts Barawa, whose squad featured a new face.

With so many matches kicking off simultaneously around London, journalists and teams were reliant on hurried text conversations with colleagues and new associates around the grounds to keep up to date – which is how the message filtered through to Bracknell's Larges Lane, where Kabylia were playing out a dire 0-0 draw with the United Koreans in Japan, that there were some question marks surrounding Barawa's new striker.

The man in question, described at the time as 'some guy who scored 25 goals last season, or something', was Mohamed Bettamer – a battering ram of a forward who scored his side's only goal in a 2-1 defeat to Cascadia. The problem? Bettamer … wasn't on squad lists. Not only had he been added to Barawa's squad after the deadline to register players, it seemed that he'd actually been added after their first match.

Uneasy rumblings became more formalised immediately after the group stage, when that 'some guy' provided a goal and an assist in the hosts' 2-0 win over Ellan Vannin – a result which eliminated the pre-tournament favourites.

The Manx side had looked fairly safe bets to go through after winning their opening games 4-1 and 2-0, but a remarkable 6-0 win for Cascadia over Tamil Eelam meant that three sides in Group A sat on six points apiece and, once CONIFA officials had finished counting on their fingers and toes, the Manxmen were out on goal difference.

Then the wrangling began.

The Manx IFA appealed the match's result on the grounds of Barawa fielding an ineligible player, only to be informed that CONIFA had granted the hosts' request to have the player registered for the tournament *after* the conclusion of their first match, and had failed to tell ... well, anyone.

As it transpired, two of Barawa's players had been told by QPR, just a few hours before kick-off in the showpiece opening match, that they could face having their contracts rescinded if they played in the tournament.

An emergency meeting was hastily scheduled for Monday's rest day, where nine members of the tournament's organising committee and representatives from the 14 other teams in the tournament voted, far from unanimously, to allow the result to stand. A second vote on whether to allow Bettamer to participate in the rest of the tournament also passed.

If CONIFA had hoped that the vote would put the matter to bed, they were sorely mistaken. A lengthy statement followed from the Manx IFA alleging that the decision to allow Bettamer to play in the tournament – contrary to CONIFA's statement – was made solely by their General Secretary rather than the organising committee as a whole, that the situation was 'manipulated' by the tournament organisers for financial reasons, in order to keep the hosts in the competition over the less traditionally marketable Manxmen.

The statement ended with calls for teams, officials and sponsors to boycott the competition in solidarity and, when no such support was forthcoming, they withdrew from the tournament three hours before their first placement match against Tibet. Not content with making their point through absence, a series of furious tweets followed, including a retweet from team captain Frank Jones, who dropped an all-caps hashtag #CORRUPT at the end of his message.

It was – if we're being reasonable about this – an absolute clusterfuck.

Speaking to Düerkop a few months after the tournament, he revealed that the situation was, somehow, even more convoluted than it seemed on the surface.

'We had a democratic vote about this in our daily tournament meeting in the team hotel,' he explained. 'Ellan Vannin presented their case, Barawa weren't there, quite an overwhelming majority decided not to overrule the result of the game, and to keep things all as they were. That, I think, is when the big mistake happened because Ellan Vannin protested against the voting decision, saying not all the teams were present – three or four were missing.

'That actually happened every day; Ellan Vannin didn't attend a single meeting before this one. There are no rules in our constitution to say that all the teams have to be there, only that they all have to be invited, which they were, and that we had to have at least six people around the table, which we did.

'The problem was that we agreed to let them have another meeting on the case, which shouldn't have happened. Part of the reason Ellan Vannin got the second meeting was that they said they had new evidence they wanted to present, and of course we needed to hear that.

'When they presented their evidence, it was a claim that the player in question was not Barawanese – whatever that means. The Barawa team said that yes, he is, he speaks Barawanese, so ... I don't want to argue on that. There is no rule in CONIFA that says you need to have an "ethnic passport" to be Barawanese or something like that; it's impossible to define.'

The point raised by Düerkop in passing is one which is likely to haunt the organisation for a long time to come. When you have an organisation made up of a diaspora of teams and people from roughly defined regions, defining player eligibility is somewhere between unfeasibly difficult and impossible.

How do you go to people who have been displaced because of wars, or people who have left everything behind them to move to another country, and ask them to prove where they came from? Then, of course, it becomes a system of 'one rule for some, another rule for others'. CONIFA is going to have to get very good at fudging things convincingly.

The very existence of the Ellan Vannin team came from a question of eligibility in the first place – or at least, a question of who truly 'represented' the island.

When there was no Manx team to be entered for the Island Games in Bermuda in 2013, now-Ellan Vannin vice president Malcolm Blackburn suggested his Manx club side, St John's United, could represent the island. The Isle of Man FA disagreed and a schism formed, leading to the Manx Independent Football Association and the Ellan Vannin team, for whom only those born on the island or who had a Manx parent or grandparent could play.

Anyway.

'That second meeting came to the conclusion, by a vote, that the new evidence was void because there was no rule that was broken. Then, the mistake was done. We should've just stuck to the first vote. Instead, we accepted to have another vote regardless of the lack of new evidence, and that vote again went in favour of Barawa.

'Ellan Vannin protested again against the vote, saying that proxy votes should not have been accepted (some teams were training while the meeting was taking place). I was not at that second meeting. Somehow, it was accepted that we should not accept proxies. I protested against that, because it was not right to tell teams that they could hand in proxies and then not accept them, so we had a third and last meeting which again went in favour of Barawa.

'I think, in general, the whole process wasn't handled well. We should've had one meeting, both teams present their case, we have a vote and if anyone protests then they need to present their new evidence before we call a second meeting. That process wasn't handled well. Otherwise, I think the result was good. All teams attended that last meeting and spoke, with very strong opinions. The decision taken was, I think, 14–6 and everyone was there and aware of the issue. I think it was a conscious decision that was taken, so I think that the end result was made in a good way after the mess before.'

Unsurprisingly, Blackburn didn't agree. Speaking on multiple Manx radio stations the morning that Ellan Vannin pulled out of the tournament, he said, 'The team, myself, everyone who has assisted Ellan Vannin in our journey over the last four years, we feel incredibly let down.

'We feel that we, as a small island, are being discriminated against because of our size – it's a lot easier to deal with an issue by ignoring us than maybe affecting the image of the tournament by dealing with the hosts.

'The tournament itself is fantastic, the standard of football has been immense. They have had the chance here to be the open, honest, and moral organisation they say they are, and they haven't shown that. They have essentially manipulated a vote and meetings to ensure that the host nation continued in this tournament.

'The lads were on such a high, and they feel like they've been cheated. And they have been cheated. Because of the way CONIFA treated us, basically with contempt, for the welfare of our players and management we decided to withdraw from the tournament with immediate effect.

'My emotion at the moment is very much that we could never be associated with this organisation again, but I have had some of the lads asking if we can continue, so we'll see what happens if things change.'

As poorly as things ended for Ellan Vannin, Barawa themselves may have come out behind in the long term.

The team – the host nation of the tournament – was hit very hard in the days following the vote. Some Manx press accused the Somali side of 'cheating' and 'tricking' CONIFA into letting them bring a ringer into their team at the last minute. Social media abuse flew around, as did rumours of the vote to expel Ellan Vannin being rigged.

Unpleasant enough at the best of times, the rumours got to the point where Barawa's quarter-final against Northern Cyprus was going to be affected. The situation led to pressure from players' families and clubs, who didn't want to be associated with a team with a reputation for cheating. A CONIFA official told me later that Bettamer received threats and 'very naughty calls' for weeks after the tournament, and was warned that his club contract could be affected.

Fortunately, that hasn't been the case for the striker, who played for both Braintree Town and Barnet FC in the months following the tournament – the latter poaching him from their National League (English fifth tier) after six goals in 15 games early in the season.

He stayed in the Barawa team for their quarter-final but, to the anger of CONIFA's executive committee, a number of his team-mates didn't. Driven out by the backlash against their win over Ellan Vannin and the fallout that followed, several Barawa squad members withdrew.

That match down in Sutton was, to be plain, a shambles. It looked like a training game, or a declassified friendly – Barawa all over the shop, Northern Cyprus trying to figure out how many goals it was okay to score without being too disrespectful to their badly depleted opponents. The match finished 8-0.

As for Ellan Vannin, they were in contact with CONIFA up to a week after the end of the tournament with a view to returning to the fold in the long term. Such a return would mean presenting a case at January 2019's AGM and being voted back in by their fellow members, but Düerkop explained in November 2018, 'We're not sure if this is going to happen, because we didn't have any follow-up. From our point of view, the ball is in their field. We took the decision and left it to them to either present a case in January or approach us earlier, which they didn't do yet.'

In true romcom style though, they came back. The motion for the Manx side's provisional expulsion to be made permanent was put to the organisation's membership at the AGM in Krakow in January 2019 after cases were made back and forth, and was rejected by 70–118, with 20 abstentions, to give the motion just 34 per cent of the available votes. To carry, it needed 75 per cent.

Ellan Vannin are back and, although they won't compete in the Euros in 2019, they will face off against a mini-Home

Nations group of hosts Yorkshire, Kernow and Jersey in the summer of 2019 for the Atlantic Heritage Cup, a tournament which will also go some way to deciding berths at 2020's World Football Cup.

That all assumes that, as they have told CONIFA, they drop the legal action that's pending. Ellan Vannin were reinstated to CONIFA at the end of January 2019, but a letter outlining plans for legal action in Sweden (where CONIFA is officially based) was received as recently as the second half of March of the same year.

The argument being made is that the expulsion in the summer was unconstitutional by CONIFA's own rules and … well, you've already got the idea. Compensation for loss of income and cover for legal costs are being sought, although CONIFA is confident of winning the case or – more likely – the case never making it to court in the first place thanks to a lack of cast-iron evidence.

No legal advisers have been brought on board by CONIFA yet, although they'll have to be sought out if the case *does* end up in front of a Swedish judge. Helpfully, two members of the organisation's executive committee – Kristóf Wenczel and Australian Kieran Pender, who ended up involved with CONIFA while in Abkhazia for the 2016 World Football Cup – are legal professionals.

It's not CONIFA's first legal challenge; a case brought by the NF-Board in Sweden was dismissed before it ever made it to a court case thanks to a Swedish system which requires a reasonably high burden of proof before a case can even be opened.

The first step is a written statement. The dispute with Ellan Vannin hasn't reached this point yet and, although CONIFA insist they're overwhelmingly confident that this isn't something they'll have to fight too hard, it could have disastrous consequences if things escalate.

Swedish legal counsel would be reasonably costly for a volunteer organisation, but the bigger problem would come if the case were to go in favour of Ellan Vannin. The number being asked for is roughly the same as CONIFA's total income for the last three years. As it was put to me by a member of the executive committee, 'If we lose the case, most likely we will be bankrupt and cease to exist.'

It would be weird if Ellan Vannin didn't drop this. Nobody in the organisation has seemed like the kind of person who'd be spiteful enough to carry through an action which would cripple the organisation they play football in, and the longer it drags on the more expensive it'll get. You ever tried to get a lawyer to write you a letter? I'd be a millionaire if I charged their word rate, I swear.

Tuvalu – Here Today…

IT'S hard to put into words Tuvalu's relative international status within the non-FIFA world without sounding dismissive of other teams – but they're in a position shared by a vanishingly small number of organisations, in that … well, their status as a state (see? status? state? Ah, you'll get it later) is not disputed.

The small group of Pacific islands became a member of the United Nations at the turn of the century and, unlike many of their CONIFA associates, they have little to worry about when it comes to political struggles or ethnic marginalisation.

The fact that the islands are about to be swallowed by the sea is a bit of a pisser though.

Let's zoom out a little.

Tuvalu is a tiny collection of islands out in the Pacific, about halfway between Hawaii and Australia – as if that gives absolutely any clue at all as to the scale of how minuscule the islands are within the context of the vast blue expanse in which they sit.

Maybe the best way to contextualise is through numbers. The Pacific Ocean is 165,200,000km², and the entire land mass of Tuvalu sits in a couple of spots – dots, really, and barely that – which amount to 26km². That's about 6,350,000 times smaller, if you don't have a calculator to hand. If you were to fly in a grid over the entire ocean, even knowing that you were looking for somewhere 'about halfway between Hawaii and Australia' ... well. You'd be looking for a *while*.

It might be that tiny, tiny landmass that means Tuvalu – despite its year-round warm weather – only sees about 2,000 tourists come to the islands each year. That's a pretty major source of potential income that just doesn't exist for the country, which is part of the reason Tuvalu has the lowest GDP of any sovereign nation in the world.

The main moneymakers aren't physical exports at all, but instead the sales of fishing licences and the leasing out of the '.tv' web domain. Food isn't particularly easy to grow on the islands, which means there's a whole lot of coconut and fish in the day-to-day diet, and imported food beyond that, with prices predictably hiked right up. It's life, but in the middle of the ocean.

The problem is, oceans are a lot like big corporations. The larger they are, the more they have a habit of making anything in 'their space' disappear without warning, mercy or a thought of paying tax. And Tuvalu is in the middle of about as hostile a takeover as you're likely to see.

Whatever your thoughts on climate change – man-made, man-assisted or a figment of the imagination of almost every single scientist and expert on the planet, possibly as part of a conspiracy for ?????? – there is one undeniable fact. Sea levels are rising, and quickly. Over the last 25 years, the global mean sea level has risen by 2.8 inches. That doesn't sound like much, but climate reports insist that a rise of as little as eight inches over the next century could make the islands uninhabitable.

Worse? That sea-level rise has been accelerating, not slowing down. Sea levels are rising 30 per cent faster than they were in the 1990s, and the lack of effective action to slow climate change globally is only hastening the potential demise of an entire country.

There's a tendency, especially in the Western world, to look at the projected maps and give a big shrug. It looks bad in countries like the UK, but on such a macro scale that it's difficult, not to care, but to wrap your head around the issue. Losing half of Liverpool and bits of Wales to the sea in 80 years sounds like the plot of a dystopian teen novel, not something that could actually happen. Day to day, there's no tangible threat to make anybody shit their pants and say 'ah, yes, actually could we maybe look at *not* putting our best efforts into melting the polar ice caps, because by the time we're underwater it's going to be a bit too late and, besides, some of Wales is basically okay at worst'.

The people of Tuvalu don't have the luxury of thinking about climate change on a macro scale. For them, this is an issue which could literally end their civilisation with a week's notice – and that tends to sharpen your focus a little.

I … look, okay, I'm not going to spend time explaining what atolls are and how little islets make up habitable land on them because you know what? I'm some bloke who usually writes about football on the internet. You've got the internet, maybe even an encyclopaedia, look it up yourself. I did. They're wicked. Educate yourself; I can't do all the heavy lifting. I'm just some bloke.

Done? Okay. Well the atoll of Funafuti is officially Tuvalu's capital. More than half of the country's population live on its 2.4km², with the main islet housing about three quarters of those in four villages, and – you get the point. A thriving metropolis this ain't.

Of course, that means that when things go wrong, they go pretty wrong. When Cyclone Pam hit Vanuatu in 2015, some 1,500km away from Tuvalu, 45 per cent of the Tuvaluan population was displaced without the storm ever coming close to reaching the islands.

The country's environment minister Soseala Tinilau – who doubles up as president of the FA, because of course he does – explained that three small islets 'were disappeared' after Pam hit half an ocean away.

'Tropical Cyclone Pam's rain bands struck Tuvalu badly,' he said, 'when the eye of the storm was situated in Vanuatu. Just imagine if the eye of the storm was in Tuvalu. If that happened, maybe all the islands would be underwater due to storm surges and coastal flooding.'

Why live in a place which could be underwater in about half the time it takes Poseidon to lift his leg and fart? Tuvalu FA General Secretary Mati Fusi Seleganiu told me, 'We don't leave the islands, because the problem we have doesn't affect only Tuvaluan people, but the whole world. Our government believes that when a problem starts to come up, we need to address what is causing it, and that it needs to be dealt with while it's still small.

'If we just leave and accept what is happening now then we are not solving the problem.

'If a virus starts in one place and the world doesn't find a cure for it, well friend, I am telling you that if we don't contain it, it's going to spread and kill the whole world.

'Our government is fighting harder than ever before to minimise the problem that is boosting climate change with the help of scientists. Data on climate will be the proof to the world that things like humans polluting the atmosphere with factories are causing the climate to change – and if we can't stop this to start saving a tiny nation like Tuvalu, then we're not gonna be able to save the world.

'To save Tuvalu is the same as saving the world.'

As long as Tuvalu exists, there *is* life, and there *are* communities, and when that happens, there tends to be football. Tuvalu's first official game was a national game at the 1979 South Pacific Games in Suva, Fiji, and it went … well, it went.

If we're not sugar-coating, it was a genuinely awful international debut. 30 August marked the birth of the Tuvalu national team on the world stage, and they announced themselves with an 18-0 defeat to Tahiti.

This was no American Samoa story, though, who famously spent years trying to revive their football team after a humiliating 31-0 defeat to Australia. A 5-3 win over Tonga the very next day restored some pride – with striker Saifoloi Metia Tealofi scoring all five – even if the following three games in the tournament saw them ship 20 goals in exchange for just seven of their own.

Erm, then they disappeared off the scene for about a quarter of a century.

It isn't especially easy to play football in Tuvalu, see. All of the teams in the country's little league do their training on the runway of the national airport because there's so little land that's a workable size, and then they have to share the Tuvalu Sport Grounds when it comes to matchday. There's precious little funding, and it's very much a 'do what you can' setup.

For all that, the Tuvalu national team is getting better. The Pacific Mini Games in 2017 was their first chance to test themselves since their admission to CONIFA the year previous and, despite a couple of thumpings, they finished fourth out of six teams – with an unprecedented two wins over FIFA-affiliated opposition. One was sat dead last in the FIFA world rankings and one was playing only Under-21s, but wins are wins, and Tuvalu won games.

It was in a buoyant mood, five months later, that Tuvalu arrived in London for the 2018 World Football Cup. Called up as late replacements for region-mates Kiribati, they faced European bronze medalists Székely Land first up – complete with the professional talents of the Fülöp brothers – before an even more intimidating clash with back-to-back European champions Padania.

'Squad preparation for the London CONIFA World Cup 2018 was not easy for us,' Mati explained. 'We did struggle and faced lots of challenges in raising funds to get money to pay for our airfares and accommodation on our way to the tournament.

'We got there thanks to our Tuvalu Government, who really supported us in paying for all our airfares and some other expenses. The journey to London wasn't easy because it was expensive, of course, but it was worth it.

'We're happy that our players were exposed to the level of football that is being played in Europe, which is completely different from the Pacific. We learned many things from this trip and we continue to work on our weaknesses and try to bring the team to the standard of football that is played in the CONIFA World Cup.'

They did come into the tournament a little under that standard. 1-0 at half-time in their opening game was more than respectable against one of the tournament favourites, but the floodgates cracked in the second half – the match finishing 4-0 – before Padania's Italian hulks pulled them to pieces and left little bits of alleged former floodgate material all over Coles Park in Haringey, to finish 8-0 winners.

Losing two matches by an aggregate score of 12-0 was about as humbling as it sounds. For all that the results essentially made sense – Padania had a former Italian and Spanish top-flight defender in their ranks, while Székely Land had real pros in their ranks – losing heavily isn't fun for anyone, especially when you have no goals to celebrate.

That left a *lot* riding on their final group game against Matabeleland, who had taken 6-1 and 5-0 thrashings from Padania and Székely Land respectively in their opening games. The southern African team won the match, but Tuvalu did score their first goal in a CONIFA-sanctioned tournament, fired home by Etimoni Timuani.

Timuani, now a lean, energetic defender, has played in Tuvalu's national team since he was a teenager, playing in the 2011 Pacific Games as a mere 19-year-old as part of a defence which conceded 20 goals in Tuvalu's five games. He didn't score, but he did catch the eye of the Tuvalu Association of Sport and National Olympic Committee, or TASNOC. Because he was fast as fuck.

When the Pacific Games rolled around again in 2015, Timuani was present again, but this time as a 100m sprinter. He wasn't just 'fast for a footballer', he was *fast*. When the stage was set for his international debut at the Games in Papua New Guinea … he false started and was disqualified. He described the experience succinctly: 'Not good.'

He'd showed enough to be his nation's leading sprinter, though, and made it to the World Championships in Beijing later that year, running a time of 11.72 seconds in his preliminary round. It wasn't enough to make the competition proper, but … well, this is quite hard to articulate, but do you have *any idea* how fast an 11.72 second 100m is? I'm a fully grown adult man who is in reasonably good shape, and I would struggle to break 15 seconds. If I spent some time training, I might be able to get that down to 14.

Being able to run that fast is a *gift*; it basically guarantees that you will be comfortably the fastest person in 99.9 per cent of rooms you ever walk into. You could look at any person in your town or city, walking down the street, and feel that smug sense of well-earned superiority. 'I can run faster than you,' you'd think, and you'd be right, because you're freakishly naturally talented and you've put the hard work in to make that mean something.

He didn't make it past the preliminary round of the World Championships. Sometimes there are freaks with better funding than you. Freaks who don't have to Google search training regimes with their coaches, pick one and follow it. Freaks whose Sport and Olympic Committee doesn't operate on a yearly budget of $10,000. Freaks whose training isn't done at the country's only airport, who don't have to balance being an international athlete with a day job working for the national pension fund.

The following summer, he went one step further in the life goal checklist, competing for Tuvalu at the 2016 Olympics in Rio. Not just competing, but competing and being the country's flag bearer at the opening ceremony. Not just being Tuvalu's flag bearer, but Tuvalu's only athlete competing in Rio in any discipline. At all.

He arrived in Brazil as the slowest of the 87 men competing in the event, and left as the joint slowest in the preliminary rounds. It didn't really matter. 'I came to expose my country, to [show] how is Tuvalu, where is Tuvalu,' he said.

That idea was backed up by Tufoua Panapa, Tuvalu's Assistant Secretary of the Ministry of Education, Youth and Sports, who said at the time, 'Right now, he's an ambassador, conveying to the world we are part of the Olympics and [part of] the world. Yes, we are looking up to [him] as someone who is displaying Tuvalu to the world, someone who has the heart to go there to compete with all the other athletes.'

Two years after his adventure in Rio, Timuani found himself displaying Tuvalu to the world once again, as an ambassador in another global competition back in London, showing off his skills and blistering pace on the left-hand side of his national football team in Haringey Borough, London, against a team who were representing a country that doesn't exist.

And he scored.

The move was a simple enough one, a ball through the midfield to midfielder Okilani Tinilau, a smart pass on the turn to thread the ball between two defenders, and a delicate finish lofted over the oncoming goalkeeper by Timuani.

Oh, and while we're at it? Tinilau went to the 2008 Olympics to run in the 100m for Tuvalu as well, meaning that the team who faced off against Matabeleland contained 28.5 per cent of the Tuvaluans ever to go to the Olympic Games.

Tinilau, a powerful figure with a tall shock of curly hair, still holds the nation's all-time records for the 100m and 200m sprints, as well as the long jump and the triple jump. Remember that one kid in school who was just so much better than everyone else at just every single sport, to the point that it was just slightly unfair? That kid who you were pretty sure could beat you, your mates and all the teachers at tiddlywinks if you gave him a chance? Tinilau is that kid, but for an entire country. An entire sovereign nation. He's a very nice man, but I think I hate him.

In the end though, despite a goal coming from two men who can run 100m in about the time it takes to down a pint and despite Katepu Iosua's heroics in saving a first-half penalty, Tuvalu fell to a 3-1 defeat in front of a majority Matabele crowd at Coles Park Stadium.

That defeat saw Tuvalu drop into the competition's placement rounds – or rather, into a worse seeding in them, as their earlier losses to Padania and Székely Land had already effectively knocked them out. Those placement rounds began with a 5-0 whomping at the hands of a United Koreans in Japan team who had failed to get going in their own group, before the Pacific Islanders faced off against Tamil Eelam in the 13–16 bracket.

The Tamil team were one of the more controversial entries in London, with the High Commission of Sri Lanka going as far as to send a letter to CONIFA president Per-Anders Blind a couple of weeks in advance of the tournament warning that their inclusion at London 2018 set a dangerous precedent.

The letter read: 'Your website states that a team called "Tamil Eelam" is taking part in your tournament this summer, and that "Tamil Eelam is an occupied state on the island of Ceylon (now called Sri Lanka)."

'I wish to bring to your attention that a territory entitled "Tamil Eelam" does not exist, nor has it existed in Sri Lanka, either de facto or de jure. It may be noted that the Liberation Tigers of Tamil Eelam (LTTE), a terrorist organisation proscribed in a number of countries including Sri Lanka, India, USA, Europe and Canada, carried out a violent campaign in the north and east of Sri Lanka in order to create a country by this name. However, their violent campaign of death and destruction, funded from abroad, was brought to an end in May 2009.

'While CONIFA proclaims in its website its vision of "enhancing global relations and international understanding", it may be noted that by including a team named "Tamil Eelam" in the tournament, it would promote and support divisive, separative tendencies as well as violence in many countries including Sri Lanka.

'The Tamil people of Sri Lanka are an integral part of the Sri Lankan society, which has overcome separatist sentiments within. The people of Sri Lanka are building a reconciled and united Sri Lanka. Therefore, inclusion of this separatist group in your tournament will only sow discord among communities of Sri Lankans living in the UK, Europe and Sri Lanka as well.'

The point the letter makes is a valid one and one which, again, CONIFA will have to face sooner rather than later. Sporting teams are a cornerstone of cultural self-representation, and they have a great deal of resonance with people. They're a flag – literally, in this case – to rally behind, and build momentum for a greater movement.

CONIFA's absolute dedication to self-determination is what has made it the organisation it is today, but the better known it becomes, the better the chances of genuinely active or ill-meaning separatist groups entering teams into their ranks for political gain.

Teams are banned from political acts or expressions while competing in CONIFA matches; any kind of goal celebration with a message written on a T-shirt under a team jersey, for example, would lead to punishments after the match, but that only takes in half the point. Regions don't *have* to pull off overt gestures on the pitch, because simply being on the pitch, on the member list, is a powerful gesture in itself. It has the potential to be a gesture saying 'we exist, and we see ourselves as something separate from you'. Some governments have recognised this – Sri Lanka's and Ukraine's not the least of them. The letter was merely another reminder of what CONIFA continues to avoid tackling head-on.

Anyway.

Tamil Eelam came from 3-1 down with five minutes remaining to win 4-3, after two goals from Tuvalu's all-time leading scorer (with eight goals) Alopua Petoa had given them a comfortable lead. When midfielder Janothan Perananthan won the match for the Tamil side in the fourth minute of injury time, the Tuvaluans collapsed, crushed. It was a hard loss to take for a team who had yet to taste even a draw at the tournament, and left them – after Ellan Vannin's expulsion from the tournament – the last placed team of all those who fulfilled their fixtures.

Their London experience wasn't over there, though, with a local team of Chagos Islands diaspora stepping in to play all of Ellan Vannin's voided games and giving Tuvalu one last chance to celebrate before they made the long, long trip back home. And boy, did they take it.

In front of around 70 people at the Bedfont Rec, Tuvalu got off to a flyer against their last-minute opponents, who had been narrowly beaten by Matabeleland two days prior. Half-time came with the score sat at 3-1, a troublingly familiar score for the members of the Tuvalu side who had been on the pitch for the Tamil Eelam turnaround, but a second half barrage secured a resounding 6-1 win – Tuvalu's biggest ever margin of victory in an international match.

And then … home, to consider the next steps. Another bid to become a FIFA member will come in the not-too-distant future, although there are still two criteria that Tuvalu fundamentally can't meet. They need a stadium with a capacity of 3,000 (twice the capacity of the Tuvalu Sports Ground, where games are played currently), and they need hotels which can house enough teams and fans for a small, CONIFA-sized tournament to be held in the country. There are neither the space nor the economic imperative for either of those things to happen.

However, taking the example of Gibraltar in Europe, FA president Tinilau suggested last year, 'I think the way forward is to work together with our Pacific neighbours, especially Fiji. If they can allow us to use Fiji as host ground for us, that would be really good. Hopefully, we can resubmit again to them and they can vote on that and see how we can go forward on that. That's the only way forward.'

The economic issue remains a big one, but FIFA – with cash reserves of around $1bn, charitable status and a stated goal of expanding the game of football – could help.

'FIFA has a lot of money,' Tinilau said, 'so why not give it to us, we build the stadium, they monitor us and if we meet their criteria, we can become members. We don't have money, we rely on the government. At the moment we are trying to upgrade our playing field back home and I also suggested an artificial surface for the new one, so I think maybe in 2019 we will have a new playing ground. Hopefully, it will meet the criteria they are looking at.'

In the short term, the goals are not as grand. The 2019 Pacific Games in Samoa are the next target, with Tinilau admitting that the CONIFA World Football Cup was a learning exercise as much as anything else, helping them prepare to take on teams from their own region in the summer.

The tournament has been used in the past for Olympic qualification, and may be again. Tuvalu can't do worse than

Micronesia in 2015 – losing all three of their games with an aggregate score of 114-0 – but they have their sights set a lot higher. With experience of international football, they're looking for wins. They might just get them.

Karpatalja – the Exiles

THERE is a shitload of Hungarian teams in CONIFA. Honestly, seriously, the entire organisation's just absolutely rammed with them, whether it's Délvidék (a Hungarian minority in northern Serbia), Felvidék (Délvidék's wacky brother if they were dwarves in *The Hobbit*, but a Hungarian minority in southern Slovakia in the meantime), Székely Land (Hungarians in Romania) or Karpatalja.

Shitloads of them. Which might not be so notable, except for the fact that they're all actually quite good – with Karpatalja the best of them all, cementing that status with a 4-2 win over Székely Land in London's World Football Cup.

That win to crown the kings of the Hungarian minorities came in the semi-finals of the tournament, a stage that not too many outside of the Karpataljan camp would have backed them to reach.

They weren't even first choices for the tournament at all, replacing Felvidék late on after a withdrawal, and then they got dumped into a group with the reigning champions Abkhazia and the team who finished third two years previously, Northern Cyprus.

It looked for all the world that the tournament debutants were on a hiding to nothing, and would be looking to play for pride in the plate competition once they were knocked out of the main tournament.

A hard-fought 1-1 draw with Northern Cyprus raised a few eyebrows on the opening day, but it was on the second matchday that Karpatalja truly announced themselves – Zsolt Gajdos giving them a 1-0 lead early against Abkhazia at Enfield, before Istvan Sandor put the icing on a 2-0 win with his second goal in two games in the 98th minute.

Sandor's goal, a delightful curled effort from 25 yards to finish a driving run, was no less than he and his side deserved. He had hit the post from close range earlier in the second half, a much easier chance than the one he eventually put away, while Zoltan Baksa came inches away from finishing the game himself with a dipping shot from range which crashed against the crossbar, leaving the frame of the goal rattling so violently that nearby earthquake detection probes registered the movement. Probably.

A rollicking 5-1 thrashing of Tibet followed to secure qualification at the top of Group B, setting up a quarter-final clash with Cascadia – and my first chance to see them in the flesh since the pre-tournament media day at the teams' hotel.

It's possible that a team produced a more professional, controlling, efficient performance somewhere else in the tournament; with at least four matches being played simultaneously around London at most kick-off times, it was impossible to get to them all and find out. But I certainly didn't see one, not against a team as dangerous and talented as Cascadia, and nor did any other journalists I asked.

The North American team came in on a real high after beating hosts Barawa 2-1 and Tamil Eelam 6-0 to secure qualification from the tournament's closest group, but they were passed and pressed out of the game by Karpatalja in the first half. The break came with the scoreline still reading 0-0, but the second half saw the Hungaro-Ukrainian side make the most of all the weaknesses they'd spent the opening 45 minutes probing – Gergő Gyürki scoring within three minutes of the restart before Ronald Takács doubled the lead just prior to the hour mark.

Cascadia pulled a goal back late on, but never looked like equalising before Gajdos scored his third goal of the tournament from the penalty spot for a 3-1 triumph, and an all-Hungarian (...ish) semi-final against Székely Land in Carshalton.

There was not a single event in the tournament like that semi-final. Not one. The Hungarian teams' fans were some of the most vocal of the tournament, turning up with flares in the colours of the Hungarian flag, banging on the sheet metal surroundings of the stands, and for the tournament to finally produce a match between two of their teams made for an electrifying spectacle.

The match lived up to it too, with a penalty saved, a penalty scored, a goalkeeping balls-up, a stunning goal, a late comeback from 3-0 to 3-2, a stoppage time counter-attack to seal a 4-2 win – everything a genuine classic could have asked for.

Status as the best Hungarian minority team in the tournament established, there was just the small matter of the final to be taken care of – on a Saturday evening in north London, with the rain spitting and splattering as Karpatalja lined up against Northern Cyprus in front of the biggest crowd ever seen at Enfield Town's Queen Elizabeth II Stadium.

The stadium itself, assuming you've never had the pleasure, has a covered terrace behind each goal, a grass bank on the far side of the pitch and changing rooms on the near – where hundreds of neutral fans and players from other CONIFA teams gathered. The bank was full of casual fans too, but the two covered stands were jam-packed, and fiercely partisan.

At one end, London's Northern Cypriot community, singing and jumping. At the other, a collection of – if we're speaking frankly – fucking terrifying massive blokes smoking cigarettes and carrying Hungarian flags, Székely flags, flags of all the teams with Hungarian representation. The message was pretty clear. Wherever you live, wherever you've settled, you're Hungarian. You're one of us.

Of course, if you *weren't* one of them, you got snarled at, asked 'Hungarian?' and pushed out of the stand when you said no, as one of my colleagues at the game discovered. Something to be said about Hungarian foreign policy there perhaps, as well as the standard-issue football partisanship, but we'll get on to that later.

The game itself was dreadful. Oh sure, the spectacle was impressive, half the pitch covered in drifting red, white and green smoke from the flares and fans at both ends really going for it, but the football was just bad. A more generous observer might have noted the intensity of the tackling, the way both teams competed in midfield, and been grateful that neither side put the game away early and destroyed the match as a spectacle, but there were few chances, no goals, and football fatigue had set in at the end of watching 13 games across six matchdays. When the match went straight to penalties at the end of 90 minutes, rather than adhere to the football tradition of 30 minutes of extra time, it was a relief.

The rain started to fall heavier as the teams made their way to the end where the Northern Cyprus fans were congregated for the shoot-out, as I and a couple of men with large cameras scampered over to get the best possible view, not just of the penalty takers themselves but of the reactions of the fans. That's the thing, in this modern age of Twitter and YouTube and streaming. You don't watch football, you watch people *watching* football.

After the first two rounds of penalties, those people watching the football looked glum. Just a year on from losing the European Football Cup final to Padania on penalties, they had seen their first two spot kicks spurned. Gyürki and György Toma, taking Karpatalja's opening pair, made no mistake.

Having taken a 2-0 lead in the shoot-out, Karpatalja did their level best to throw it away – missing their next two penalties – while Northern Cyprus's third and fourth takers made amends for earlier mistakes. From a position of near-total dominance, they'd let things slip, and the shoot-out was level once again. Sudden death. Alex Svedjuk defied the stand full of baying Northern Cypriot fans in front of him to give Karpatalja the advantage, and left Béla Fejér standing in goal to face Halil Turan, Northern Cyprus's leading scorer in the tournament with five goals.

Turan fired to the goalkeeper's right, only to watch on as Fejér guessed right and pushed the ball around the post with both hands. A moment of pure, crystallised silence, ended by a roar of frustration from the fans behind the goal. Watching the footage back, it took Fejér a couple of seconds to realise just what he'd done, standing up from his dive and giving an understated fist pump, before his synapses fired and he took off at full sprint down the pitch, tearing his sodden shirt off as he ran and twirling it around his head in victory.

Karpatalja, the last-minute call-up to the tournament, the team who *were never meant to be there*, were CONIFA world champions.

The pitch was invaded instantly, fans and players celebrating together, jumping, cheering, chanting and singing. Fans with T-shirts, scarves and flags of Székely Land or Sepsi OSK, the first Székely team to reach the top tier of Romanian football, had their arms around players' shoulders. The message, intended or not, was clear. You are Hungarian before you're Ukrainian, and for that we'll celebrate with you.

The party at the hotel where 13 of the 16 teams were staying went on long into the night, and into the next morning for some teams. While a number of staff and players – and a few journalists – were nursing hangovers the following morning, a far larger story was developing in the background, one which would break the following day.

Barely 36 hours after Karpatalja's players had one of the great moments of their football lives, their lives became a lot more complicated, and dangerous. Ukraine's sports minister, Igor Zhdanov, took to his official Facebook page to call for the team to be 'interrogated', accusing them of a 'frank act of sporting separatism'.

He wrote, 'I call on the Security Service of Ukraine to respond appropriately to such a frank act of sporting separatism. It is necessary to interrogate the players of the team, as well as to analyse in detail the activities of the deputy organiser of the "Carpathian" [the Karpataljan team] for the purpose of encroachment on the territorial integrity of Ukraine and ties with terrorist and separatist groups.'

The same day, Ukraine's football federation released a statement along similar lines, promising to apply harsh sanctions to the players, ban them from amateur and professional football in the country and actively called for criminal investigations.

To quote, 'According to the results of this review, sanctions will be applied against these players, in particular, disqualification, after which players will not be able to claim to participate in amateur or professional tournaments held on the territory of Ukraine under the auspices of the FFU {Football Federation of Ukraine].

'We also urge the law enforcement agencies of Ukraine to pay attention to the fact of participation of the indicated players in competitions organised by CONIFA and to check their actions on the subject of propaganda of separatism and encroachment on the territorial integrity and inviolability of Ukraine.'

It's worth saying at this point that there were no separatist incitements by the Karpataljan players in London, and they wore the flag of their Ukrainian region as part of their shirt design. But there's always a 'but'.

Events like CONIFA's World Football Cup don't occur in a vacuum. As much as CONIFA have maintained, and still maintain, that their stance is one of strict non-politicism, that … isn't how politics works. That's not how a *lot* of things work. Just because you say something – even if you mean it as you say it, and believe fully that it's what you're doing – that doesn't make it true.

It's a theme that's repeated again and again through the ranks of CONIFA. The sheer existence of a team representing part of a country *as a separate entity* is going to be felt differently in different contexts. Great Britain isn't threatened by the idea of a Yorkshire team angling for a little cultural representation, because the country is stable – there is no nationalist movement and no recent history of violent separatism.

The USA and Canada aren't cracking down on the idea of a Cascadia team representing the region at an international event because, again, there's nothing that suggests that the recognition of the bioregion of Cascadia is a threat to the political and structural integrity of their respective countries.

And then ... Ukraine; Ukraine, which lost control of swathes of its territory, not just in living memory, but in the last five years. February 2014 saw, essentially, a revolution in the country, with elections brought forward and billionaire oligarch Petro Poroshenko becoming president. The cities Donetsk and Luhansk declared their independence after the revolution and, at time of writing, are still occupied by revolutionary forces and are still at war with Ukrainian forces over the territory.

Those revolutionary forces, crucially, have been backed by Russian paramilitary groups, something which the head of the Ukrainian Security Service described as tantamount to a direct invasion of Ukrainian territory by Russia.

Unhappiness in Donetsk, and some Russian concern over the state of Ukraine after the 2014 revolution, were to be expected. Deposed president Viktor Yanukovych is a former governor of the region, which lies close to the Russian border, and spent much of his time as president strengthening Ukrainian ties with Moscow.

The reaction was almost immediate. Barely a month after the end of February's revolution, the 'Donetsk People's Republic' was declared and fighting began. In the least shocking turn of events ever, civilians became collateral damage – the most internationally renowned incident being the downing of Malaysia Airlines Flight 17, and the deaths of all 298 passengers and crew on board. The missile which hit the plane was fired from a rebel-controlled area of Donetsk and, investigators later determined, was brought from Russia to Ukraine on the morning of the attack. The launcher returned the next day.

The UN Office of the High Commissioner for Human Rights estimated in February 2019 that, about five years into the conflict, around 13,000 lives have been lost, more than 3,300 of those being civilians.

Outside influence on rebels and separatists, then, is an ongoing concern for the increasingly paranoid Ukrainian government.

All the while, Hungary's far-right Prime Minister Viktor Orban has been an agitator from behind his own borders, saying in an address to the Hungarian parliament during the 2014 revolution, 'Hungarians in the Carpathian basin have the right to dual citizenship, community rights and autonomy. This is the position which we will represent in the international political arena.'

That 'Carpathian basin' refers to the region represented by Karpatalja. Orban and Hungary's agitations haven't stopped there, calling the Ukrainian government 'anti-Hungarian' in 2018 as political fighting continues.

It's in that context, then, that Ukraine's actions in October 2018 must be viewed. All players and members of the Karpataljan staff with Ukrainian passports were banned from football in Ukraine for life, while those with Hungarian citizenship – most of the squad, despite being born in Ukraine – are banned from entering the country at all.

As CONIFA's open letter to the Ukrainian President read, 'The overwhelming majority of those players have family and friends in Ukraine. Others, like the coach Istvan Sandor, can now never again visit the graves of their parents and, in his case, his brother. Mr Sandor is also quoted by several

Hungarian newspapers claiming that the team "brought victory [in the World Football Cup, 2018] to Karpatalja and the whole of Ukraine."'

Since their denouncement, the team, who I found open and pleasant in London, have refused to speak to me. I've reached out multiple times directly, through CONIFA and intermediaries, but the answer has been the same. 'We're not making things worse for ourselves.'

I spoke to Dr Alex Clarkson, a lecturer in German and European studies at King's College London, in the weeks after October's denouncement, who explained, 'The gist of my view on this is that the Ukrainian government is very sensitive to any sign of separatist sentiment in Ukrainian regions, particularly since at the same time it is going through a process of administrative decentralisation.

'With most other regions, including those with big minorities, local powerbrokers and neighbouring governments have had arguments with Kyiv but everything has been handled in a pretty straightforward and non-escalatory manner because there is enough trust on all sides. With Zakarpattia the problem is that Orban has a track record of stoking Hungarian minority resentment, not just in Ukraine, but also in Romania and Slovakia.

'His regular attempts to control the development of the communities in Zakarpattia and blackmail Ukraine through blocking NATO and EU processes over a (admittedly botched) Ukrainian language education bill has only heightened Ukrainian state sensitivity. Throw in his rhetoric over Zakarpattia during the Crimea crisis in 2014 and his repeated toying with Putin, and Kyiv is downright paranoid about what Budapest is up to. And I would argue not without reason.

'So while this is a huge and harmful overreaction by the Ukrainian government, it has to be placed in the context of years and years of messing around by Orban and his various local allies. Not just in ways that annoy Kyiv, but also in ways that have come to seriously irritate local powerbrokers in the region, like the Baloha brothers, some of which may well be in a Hungarian minority but still have a strong stake in the survival of the Ukrainian state and the seamless integration of it into European-level institutions.

'These football players are paying the price of Orban's careless meddling and Ukraine's security paranoia in response to it.'

The 'Crimea crisis' he mentions is another strand to the 2014 revolution and the fallout from it, when Russia directly – not indirectly, through 'Russian nationals' not connected to the government, but directly – annexed Crimea.

President Vladimir Putin defends the move to 'assist' Crimea in its brief, successful (although as yet not internationally recognised) independence movement as merely supporting 'self-determination'. In the years since, Crimea has been almost entirely taken into Russia, with Russian media and a security fence now separating the territory from the rest of Ukraine. To all intents and purposes, Crimea is functionally Russian. Again, Ukraine is on the highest of high alerts against what they see as outside interference in any of its territories.

Part of the players' concern when they refuse to speak now is straightforward. The more attention is drawn to them, whether personally or as a collective, the more public their participation in the issue is and the less likely those in Ukraine who oppose their return will be to quietly back down – hence the refusal to speak even anonymously.

Another part, though, is more insidious. Some team members' names appeared on Myrotvorets, a website revealing personal information of people deemed to be 'enemies of Ukraine'. The database is maintained by the Security Service of Ukraine, and includes thousands of journalists, whose phone numbers, email addresses and even personal addresses were published on the site – with pro-Russian Ukrainian writer Oles Buzina and politician Oleg Kalashnikov shot dead near and at their homes respectively within days of their home addresses being posted in 2015. No definitive link between the Myrotvorets posts and the assassinations was ever proved, but the timeline was enough to give pause to anyone whose details have appeared on the website.

Karpatalja – or Zakarpattia – was coming under increased scrutiny in Ukraine at the end of 2018, with the denouncement of the football team in October coinciding to within days with the addition of 300 government and local officials from the area who had obtained Hungarian passports while living in Ukraine.

More political dick waving followed, Hungarian Minister of Foreign Affairs and Trade Peter Szijjarto responding to the fresh listings of 'alleged' Hungarian citizens by claiming then-President Poroshenko 'gave his consent to the hate campaign in an attempt to increase his popularity'.

None of this, of course, has helped or will help the people caught in the middle of the storm. For the time being at least, the Karpatalja team will continue to pay a high price for something as simple as representing their people in a football tournament. As hardliners on the two sides become more entrenched in their views, and Ukraine becomes more fiercely protective of its territory, relations are unlikely to become less frosty.

CONIFA's World Football champions are exiles.

* * * *

In the time since most of this chapter was written, the situation has escalated further. The SBU, Ukraine's counter-intelligence and terrorism force, have, to use their wording, 'announced a suspicion of high treason' to a district council official of the Karpatalja region for his part in the creation of the football team.

Multiple Ukrainian news outlets reported that Tibor Feesh was under 'pretrial investigation' by the SBU, which showed that he organised the team's entry into the World Football Cup – or as one report had it, 'organised the participation of the fake "Transcarpathian team" in the so-called "unrecognised republics" football championship'.

The case against the official appears to centre around his off-field activities to help the team get to London, including helping to procure their shirts (one of which was in the colour of the Ukrainian flag), and promoting the team's participation in the tournament. This, the security services claim, 'created a threat to the national integrity of the state'.

The last two paragraphs of the report are, I think, worth reproducing in full to reinforce the seriousness with which this case is being taken.

'The staff of the Security Council of Ukraine found out that in the unrecognised championship, athletes performed in uniform with a combined logo of the coat of arms, flag, contour map of the Transcarpathian region, combined with the state symbols of the neighbouring European country. According to the conclusions of experts, the emblem of the fake team contained symbols that can be interpreted as declaring claims and encroachments on the territorial integrity of Ukraine.

'Investigators of the Office of the SBU in the Transcarpathian region for the deliberate actions of the deputy of the district council to the detriment of the sovereignty, territorial integrity, immunity and information security of our state announced to him suspicion of committing a crime under Part 1 of Art. 111 of the Criminal Code of Ukraine. The pretrial investigation continues.'

For those who are curious (I was), Part 1 of Article 111 of the Ukrainian Criminal Code reads as follows. 'High treason, that is an act wilfully committed by a citizen of Ukraine in the detriment of sovereignty, territorial integrity and inviolability, defence capability, and state, economic or information security of Ukraine: joining the enemy at the time of martial law or armed conflict, espionage, assistance in subversive activities against Ukraine provided to a foreign state, a foreign organisation or their representatives.

'It shall be punishable by imprisonment for a term of ten to 15 years.'

Getting in touch with anyone to do with the team is incredibly difficult as things stand, and Ukrainian reports are vague, but Feesh is currently in hiding in Budapest after Ukraine called in Interpol (presumably the worldwide police cooperation body, not the New York post-punk revival band) in an effort to get him deported. The Hungarian foreign ministry have taken over his case and the government are dealing with it directly, with Orban holding at least one conversation with a Ukrainian official about the case.

Going back to Ukraine isn't an option for Feesh. He appears to have, by and large, done the things he's being accused of – providing the team with kit, gathering some support for them, helping them enter the tournament – although not all of them, having also been accused of 'tricking' the players into supporting a separatist ideal in playing for the team.

However, the Karpatalja team was never meant as an expression of separatist ideals. This was meant to be a simple effort made by a group to create a little heritage for themselves from their new homes, combining the old and the new without creating division. To call that high treason is the grossest of overreactions, the Ukrainian state coming down with a ten-ton hammer when something gentler, something more accepting, could have served the situation.

Ukraine isn't solely to blame for that reaction. Orban must shoulder a lot of the responsibility for the environment he has created for Hungarian-Ukrainian people, and the constant niggling at Russia into Ukrainian territory has done massive amounts to foster paranoia and distrust of the expression of anything other than pure, unadulterated Ukrainian nationalism.

Ukraine's history makes that difficult. As recently as 1990, the country was part of the USSR. Before that, there was a history of being part of Russia, a partner of Russia, a state independent of Russia … the point being, Ukraine has hardly been stable as an independent state or nation for some time. Even in the mid-2000s, there was a peaceful revolution in protest of a 'rigged' election and the poisoning of a prime ministerial candidate. The country barely goes a decade without large public upheaval. It is not, to the untrained eye, a state designed to remain whole in the long term. How can it be?

There will be elections in the spring of 2019. Things may change. Nationalist sentiment, at least to a large extent, is unlikely to. At time of writing, the leading candidate – ahead in all the polls – is a comedian who has played an unlikely winning presidential candidate on television. Ukraine has a way to go.

The view of CONIFA? 'Morally you always feel responsible if something like this happens. Technically it doesn't really change our view on being non-political, though – it strengthens our argument. The team *was* non-political, they embraced Ukraine and Hungary and there wasn't much more they could do to prove that they weren't trying to stir up trouble. We don't feel like we have been political by allowing Karpatalja to play.'

CONIFA's World Football champions are, still, exiles.

Northern Cyprus –
Always the Bridesmaids

N ORTHERN Cyprus? Turkish-occupied Cyprus? The top half of a miasmatic clusterfuck of an island unofficially split between Greece, Turkey and people who'd quite like to just be left alone to live their lives?

The Northern Cyprus football federation (the Kibris Türk Futbol Federasyonu, or KTFF) is among the oldest in CONIFA's ranks, its history spanning for generations before a reindeer herder and a German shirt collector met at a summit.

The KTFF was formed all the way back in 1955 as Turkish Cypriot clubs began to withdraw from general Cypriot sporting activities, although they didn't play together as a 'national team' for seven years, making their debut as a collective in 1962 under the name of 'Turkish Cypriots' (and getting spanked 5-0 by Turkey), a full dozen years before the effective partition of the country in 1974 – which meant that being from the north wasn't actually a requirement for membership of the playing staff, just … being a Turkish speaker.

See how I'm doing all the maths for you so you don't have to work out which year things happened in by adding up the gaps, by the way? I'm a darling. Thank me later.

Of course, then came the war and the partition and the unpleasantness. The Autonomous Turkish Cypriot Administration was formed in 1974 after a Greek Cypriot coup prompted the Turkish government to send their own army over to the island, ostensibly to protect the Turkish Cypriots living there, and invaded en masse, taking around 35 per cent of the island.

Negotiations continued, and continued to fail – as did the original coup – with the idea of a Turkish Federated State of Cyprus being rejected by both Cyprus and the UN in 1975. Political machinations continued on in the background (and foreground) for years, with a Turkish Cypriot football team going to the Islamic Games in 1980 and getting beaten by Turkey (again) 5-0 (again). They did manage one win in the tournament, though, balancing a 2-0 defeat to Saudi Arabia and a 1-1 draw with Libya with a 2-1 victory over Malaysia.

The landscape changed drastically in 1983, when Northern Cyprus (or, rather, the Turkish Republic of Northern Cyprus) unilaterally declared independence from the rest of the country. Cyprus and the UN (again) rejected that claim of independence. That declaration ended an agreement that the KTFF had reached with FIFA to allow them to play games against other FIFA-affiliated countries, leaving the team somewhat in the wilderness internationally.

Since then, the majority of Turkish Cypriot players, especially those capable of playing at a reasonably high level, have gone to play for clubs in Turkey – unsurprising given the closeness of their relationship.

The Northern Cyprus team faded away from the (relative) limelight at that point, a lack of organised non-FIFA football and the region's political isolation leaving fixtures few and far between until the turn of the millennium.

Just a brief aside before we jump back into Northern Cyprus's return to the international stage at the start of the 21st century; the internet's bloody brilliant, isn't it? It's no coincidence that the emergence of organisations like the NF-Board and CONIFA have coincided with the internet going from a bog-slow 'dial-up in reasonably wealthy places' thing to something more functional and widely available worldwide in the early 2000s.

Rather than having to scour phone listings, post letters and go to places without any idea of what you were going to find at the other end, it became possible to spend ten minutes pinging off an email. Rather than having to spend ages hunting down the phone number of someone you'd never talked to in a different country, you could Google (well, AltaVista or Ask Jeeves) them. Maybe they'd have a website!

Websites and forums became rallying points for fans of … well, everything. For me, it was Spurs (not sure why – I'm a Spurs sympathiser but a Carlisle fan) and pop-punk music forums. And they were *everywhere*.

It took ten minutes to set up a little ProBoards forum for your particular interest and then bam, there it was, you were the owner of a little domain where people could talk about that thing, and if they wanted, organise around it. The Punktastic message boards (RIP) had thousands of active members around the country, forming bands and going to gigs off the back of conversations online. The internet made widespread organisation so much easier.

It was in front of that backdrop that Northern Cyprus returned to organised international football in 2004, when the NF-Board was founded and went on the hunt for members. The KTFF 50th Anniversary Cup was played under the NF-Board's banner the following year, a three-team league tournament which saw the hosts come out on top against Kosovo and Sapmi, beating the now-FIFA members 1-0 and thrashing Sapmi 6-2 in North Nicosia.

The 2006 editions of the FIFI Wild Cup (see Tibet's chapter for a fuller account of *that* particular stunt) and the ELF Cup were both won by Northern Cyprus, but the former hinted at a theme that would become incredibly, painfully familiar to Turkish Cypriot fans a decade or so later. A tight, cagey knockout match – in this case the final against Zanzibar – followed by a penalty shoot-out.

Three tournament triumphs in 18 months left the Northern Cypriots right at the top of the non-FIFA tree, which, of course, meant that they then didn't play another tournament match for six years.

When they did return, it was for the 2012 VIVA World Cup in Iraqi Kurdistan, the NF-Board's last world tournament before they became defunct. Despite a defeat to French side Provence in the group stage, a thumping 15-0 win over Darfur meant that the Cypriots progressed to the semi-finals as the leading runners-up, where they beat Zanzibar to set up a final with the hosts.

They lost. They didn't make it to CONIFA's first World Football Cup, but they did turn up for the second – beating Padania for the bronze medal after losing to the hosts (another phrase that's come up a couple of times) in the semi-finals.

There would be no losing to the hosts the following summer, when Northern Cyprus welcomed seven other teams to Nicosia, Kyrenia, Famagusta and Morphou for the 2017 European Football Cup. The group stage was competitive, but the hosts went through unbeaten – beating Karpatalja and South Ossetia before sealing top spot with a 0-0 draw against Abkhazia.

Halil Turan struck in both the semi-final (to snatch a late 2-1 win over Székely Land) and the final, but his goal against Padania in the latter match was only enough to force a penalty shoot-out. The Italians held their nerve. The Cypriots didn't, and lost 4-2 from the spot on home soil in Nicosia. They'd grabbed a medal for the third time in three tournaments, but not a gold one.

And so to London in the summer of 2018. A 2011 Home Affairs Committee report estimated that there are around 300,000 people of Turkish Cypriot origin resident in the UK, which you might recognise as being 'more people than are living in Northern Cyprus, total'. With the World Football Cup coming to London, where the majority of those Turkish Cypriots live, there was no shortage of partisan local fans. No shortage of pressure, either.

Billy Mehmet took no time at all to ease a little bit of that pressure, putting Northern Cyprus ahead after just 13 minutes of their opening group game against Karpatalja in Enfield. Istvan Sandor equalised and the match finished 1-1, but the marker had been laid down. In a high-quality game, the beaten European finalists were physically competitive and talented.

A hulking striker, tall and well built, Mehmet was a new addition to the squad from the previous summer – and possibly the most high profile.

He's played on three continents, scored goals on all of them, and captained West Ham's prestigious Academy of

Football as a youngster. He played six times for the Republic of Ireland's Under-21s and, yes, does have a list of potential passports as long as his arm.

Mehmet's qualification for the Irish national team came through his grandmother on his mother's side, having been born in London to an Irish-English mother and a Turkish Cypriot father. After a solid dozen years in the West Ham setup, he left at the age of 18 after failing to break into a first team which contained, the season he left, the likes of Jermain Defoe, Marlon Harewood, Bobby Zamora and my sometime Love Sport Radio colleague David Connolly.

Just to add another bit of Britain to his CV, he went north – spending seven years in Scotland with Dunfermline and St Mirren, before a total of 44 goals and assists in his final two seasons north of the border caught the eye. That's when he swapped climates and went to Turkey. Then, erm, Australia. And Malaysia. And Singapore.

It wasn't until he was in his 30s and, theoretically, the twilight of his career that he moved out to Northern Cyprus with Alsancak Yesilova, going out to connect with his father's country for the first time in his career.

'I'm a little bit gutted,' he admitted to football website Goal at the World Football Cup in London. 'I could have played for them a long time ago. The only problem was that I didn't really know about the team – this is my first year with them.

'As London is my home town, when they chose me to play it was perfect. I always said that I would love to play for the country in which my dad was born. Not only that, but to play in the country in which we were brought up is ideal. So it's a proud moment for me and a proud moment for my dad as well.'

While the tournament and the team clearly meant a lot to Mehmet, the grander meaning behind the team was a little lost on him. In a way, he was the CONIFA ideal – someone who felt a connection to a culture they wouldn't otherwise be able to represent, and someone who is admittedly pretty blank on the political situation.

'When I first moved to Cyprus I heard they were trying to amalgamate the North and South Cypriot teams, but I don't know what's going on there. There seems to be a lot of politics involved, which I don't know much about.

'Of course, it would be great if they teamed up, but if they don't then we'll keep entering competitions like this, and hopefully keep doing well and keep getting recognised, and then maybe one day it'll happen.'

Of the teams currently competing under the CONIFA banner, Northern Cyprus are one of the more likely to gain some kind of FIFA recognition at some point, whether that comes from joining up with the Cyprus team currently under FIFA and UEFA's auspices or as a team in their own right. 'More likely' doesn't mean *actually* likely, though, and there's a whole athletics stadium's facilities room worth of hurdles to clear before anything like that could happen.

Speaking of stadiums, the World Football Cup Final was nearly held in a different one; and the fact that it wasn't is entirely down to Northern Cyprus's presence. Talks had been ongoing for months about the possibility of holding the final at The Hive, Barnet FC's ground, which had hosted two FIFA internationals in the past.

A 6,500-capacity stadium not a million miles away from the hotel the teams were staying at, a really professional complex built for a fully professional football team: it was perfect.

The deal, I was told by someone close to the conversation at CONIFA, was as good as signed. Unfortunately, someone on one end or the other hadn't done 100 per cent of their research. Barnet's chairman and owner Anthony Kleanthous's parents came over from Cyprus – that is to say, Greek Cyprus – before he was born, and the idea of staging a tournament final which could (and in the end *did*) feature Northern Cyprus at his stadium was a no-go.

In the end, the only time The Hive featured anywhere near the tournament was for Cascadia's first training session, booked through the time-honoured tradition of 'knowing someone who knows someone'. Nothing untoward, of course, because CONIFA had nothing to do with it.

The Cypriot government also wrote to a number of councils ahead of the tournament, warning them that – for political reasons, to risk legitimising a non-legitimate 'state' – they shouldn't host World Football Cup matches. Whether Northern Cyprus were due to play in that council was irrelevant.

Obviously those 'warnings' weren't heeded and the tournament went ahead as planned, something which delighted Orcun Kamali, vice president of the KTFF. A man who's been on every side of Northern Cypriot football, Kamali has been involved with the FA for a decade now, trying to give the next generation the chance to play football wherever they want.

The idea of 'the next generation' comes up over and over again when we talk – although he's a man for whom the concept of conversation is pretty free-form anyway, questions being answered with completely unrelated sentences, thoughts being interrupted by a screeching handbrake turn mid-sentence to a completely different topic.

Through all that though, it's clear that he knows the project of getting Northern Cyprus into any kind of FIFA situation is a long-term one, and one that he hates having to explain to kids who are a generation removed from the island's split.

'Because of the FIFA regulations, we aren't a member of FIFA because of the Cyprus political issue. This is very, very, very bad for us. It's unbelievable. We always say there's no politics in the football, but there's no answer to give our youth players and the children to say "you can't play football" that makes sense for them.

'So this is the only way we can make a national team, to play for CONIFA.'

Unlike a number of the teams they're competing against in CONIFA, the KTFF have been around a long time. A very long time. There's a professional league structure in Northern Cyprus with a 16-team Super League and First Division for both seniors and Under-21s, leagues for Under-17s, Under-15s and a women's football setup, and Kamali proudly notes, 'We're starting to organise a futsal league with university clubs.'

The setup is impressive, although it has its drawbacks. The main one is, surprise surprise, related to FIFA's refusal to recognise either the Northern Cyprus national team or domestic league structure under its auspices.

Not to go into too much of the detail, the short version is that clubs are usually protected from players just up and leaving by FIFA's rules, which would impose sanctions on individuals in breach of their club contracts. Nobody's going to up and leave a club if they're banned from playing in a FIFA-sanctioned league (i.e. almost all of them) once they do it.

The key word in the parentheses above? 'Almost.' Northern Cyprus's league isn't recognised by FIFA, so players can skate out of their deals when another club comes calling and there's precious little that the Cypriot clubs can do about it. There are exceptions and asterisks and all the rest of it, but that's essentially it.

'We are not a member [of FIFA], Kamali continues, so it's not easy for us; we can't play against the FIFA members. FIFA only accept the Greek Cypriot FA on the island so while we have foreign players, it's complicated. Sometimes they go away and leave without saying anything to their club, but we can't go to FIFA to ask for our rights to be protected because we aren't a member.

'So we make a deal with the players, we have three foreign players for each team – very qualified players – and they get a very good salary. They stay here; sometimes they use us as a passage if they can't find a team to play for. They have time to play; it's a good choice for them to come here. Instead of not playing football, you play football. You keep your fitness up.'

Just as FIFA membership eludes the northern half of the island, so does membership to the EU. Kind of. A bit.

Cyprus, as a whole, was approved for EU membership in 2004 with hopes that the governments in the north and south could reach a settlement agreement for reunification – the EU recognising only the government of the south for the time being, leaving the north on the outside looking in.

The north voted to support reunification. The south, having been told that they would become EU members, whether as part of a united *or* divided island, did not. Ascension to EU status was an awkward hotchpotch of half-granted rights and half-applied laws. The whole island is part of the EU, but the north is exempt from its laws and legislation because it's under the control of a non-recognised government.

The Turkish lira remains the official currency in the north, while the south trades in the euro. It's … complicated, and not looking like untangling easily any time soon. Politics, eh? Let's get back to the football.

Yenicami Agdelen is the northern half of the island's pre-eminent club in recent years, winning four of the last five Super Lig titles and providing four players for the national team – no single team providing more, inside or outside of the league.

Now, those players *mostly* come from inside the league. One teenage defender in the squad for London 2018, Necati Gench, plays in Northern Cyprus for non-league side Yeni Boğaziçi. Only one other member of that 2018 team plays abroad: Ahmet Sivri, one of Northern Cyprus's brightest prospects and an exciting young goalscorer for the Under-21 side of reigning Turkish champions Galatasaray.

Sivri is at a crucial stage in his development as a player; 19 years old and with a full season of Under-21s football under his belt, he's close to having to make the step up to the first team at one of Turkey's biggest clubs or having to drop down the table to forge a career. His numbers for the Under-21s and his performances for Northern Cyprus, though, as well as his two games for Turkey's Under-19s, hint at a bright future.

Kamali is clearly proud of the work that the KTFF has done in unearthing some of the emerging talent, saying, 'We have a couple of players who play in Turkey as well, Ahmet at Galatasaray – they're young but they have a future.

'We mostly try to participate [as a national team], but it's not easy because we live on an island, so transport is a

Cascadia's goalkeepers work out in their first training session

Ellan Vannin and Cascadia line up for their World Football Cup opener

A nattily dressed Cascadia fan, who was everywhere

*Stefano
Tignonsini
walks out
for Padania
against
Matabeleland*

*Matabeleland
players thank their
fans after a 6-1
defeat to Padania*

*Dignity in
defeat*

Matabele players and coaches pray ay Sutton after their first game

Tuvalu parade their national flag at the World Football Cup opening ceremony

A Tibetan singer performs for the world at London's opening ceremony

The man, the myth, the legend. Mark Clattenburg emerges from the tunnel

Tamil Eelam's team line up for the tournament's showcase opener

A Kabylia fan bonds with United Koreans of Japan supporters in Bracknell

*Byun Yeong-jang of
Tokyo United and UKJ
warms up*

*Kabylian fans
turn a football
match into a
cultural festival
in Bracknell*

Bruce Grobbelaar, fiery as ever at 60

Defeat for Tuvalu against
Matabeleland

Cascadia captain James Riley talks to
the media in the dusk

The World
Football
Cup Final
started in
showy styl

Hungarians for Hungarians at the WFC Final

What's football without flares?

Northern Cyprus fans at the World Football Cup Final

A Karpatalja coach. His tattoo reads 'Every Hungarian is responsible for every Hungarian'

Haircut of the tournament, and it wasn't close

VIP seats? Tuvalu players watch the final from the stadium's roof

Triumphant. Karpatalja's shootout hero Béla Fejér celebrates with Hungarian fans after a pitch invasion

problem for us. It depends where the games are, because it's not easy to play matches if there's not a big event involved. To just go and play one match isn't very responsible for us, it's going to be a lot of money to come and go, and our budget is not very big.'

Maybe the biggest boost for young Sivri going into future tournaments with Northern Cyprus is the part he *didn't* play in the final in London, or on home soil in 2017. If there's one thing English football fans know, it's the effect that losing crucial penalty shoot-outs can have on the psyche of a player and of a nation; but Sivri wasn't called upon to step up from 12 yards against Karpatalja.

No Gareth Southgate, him. Being untainted by the failures of the generation that came before you is a boost – just look at the England team who finally won a major penalty shoot-out just a few weeks after London 2018, at the FIFA World Cup in Russia. None of the players who scored had even played in a major tournament game that had ended in a shoot-out until that point. (The one who had, Jordan Henderson, came on as a late sub against Italy in 2012. He didn't take a penalty, but England did lose.)

On the other hand, maybe that's a particularly English phenomenon, something that happens to the kind of country that spends every waking moment staring wide-eyed into the fragility of its own collective psyche, the kind of country that longs with barely disguised hunger to completely collapse, the kind of country that can't go to a single sporting event without at least two separate crises.

When the shoot-outs came up in conversation with Kamali, he was … not very English about them. 'This is football, Chris! You can't win always, but that's why we play. We are playing, we show our football, our talented young people, our love of the game. We love football in Northern Cyprus. You know how many clubs we have here?'

At this point he breaks off to do some ad hoc maths down the phone line, at once entirely baffling and deeply entertaining. 'It's about 120. 150? Something like that.'

That point not settled in the slightest, he bulldozes on, 'The participation to play football internationally is exciting; it's very good for us. We can compare our football with the world.'

In addition to his role as the KTFF's vice president, Kamali is responsible for the board's foreign relations. A player at a high level in the Northern Cypriot league system himself in his youth, he's made it his mission over the last decade to make sure that the next generation, and the ones after, can play football without having to worry about being limited by the politics that came before.

'This is voluntary,' he laughs, 'but I spend a lot of time here. I've been here for ten years. I was a football player, I was a coach, I was a club director. I have directly suffered from not being able to play internationally.

'I have good relationships with football clubs here, and education about football, so I said to myself that I will be part of the governance to help the future, the next generation, to be able to play the football I wasn't.

'Do you know that the new generation can play football on computers? They can chat, they can talk, they can do everything, all over the world. My son is asking me "why can't we play football against these people? I'm playing with my friends from England, from Japan; why can't we play football with them?"

'How can you explain that to a 12-year-old boy? That it's all because of politics? It's a shame for football. You can't say to young people "you can't play football". Football is one language. Same regulations, same rules. Same language.'

This comes back, again, to the point about the internet providing a rallying point for the regionalised, marginalised by the international football community. Sitting at home, playing FIFA on the Xbox, running through their hundreds and hundreds of teams and not seeing your own as an option? You're going to want to know why.

Once you know why – and again, the internet exists, so that's not hard – you start to think about that. Whether you can do something about it, whether it's something you want to accept. Awareness breeds change, slowly but surely.

'It's still my dream to see the world's teams come here and play football with our young people.

'I'm not talking about the politics of the island; I don't care. Our clubs were established before the Cypriot Republic, when the English still governed here, and they still exist now. They're playing football. And now we're saying that because of politics you can't play internationally? Even the clubs? Even in friendlies?

'Tell me, in sports, if you can't compete how will you improve? It's a shame for football. We can't put borders up for young people not to play football. With their mobiles and their iPads, they can reach everywhere. But on the pitch? They can't.

'CONIFA is giving us a chance to play.'

Chagos Islands – Sagren

IF you go to the Chagos Islands, you won't find any Chagossians. You'll find some Americans with guns, you'll find some donkeys, and you'll find coconut crabs (which you should Google, but only if you've got an hour or two set aside afterwards to spend cursing whatever god or deity you believe in for putting us on the same island as these freak alien abominations).

You'll find one of the most diverse ecological environments in the world. But you won't find any Chagossians. That's because, to use a line occasionally grumbled by an Irish colleague, 'the Brits are a bunch of bastards'.

The islands were colonised by the British – not a great surprise; that's happened quite a lot historically – as was Mauritius, about 300 miles north. Mauritius, though, ended up more or less ruling over the Chagos Islands, before handing them back to British control shortly before they themselves became an independent state in 1968.

Then Britain leased out the newly formed 'British Indian Ocean Territory', essentially the Chagos Islands, to the USA for the next 50 years. To use as a military base. Good. The issue that you come up against when selling off an island you claim to own is that, a lot of the time, people live on those islands and don't like the idea that the land they live on is being handed over to have a bunch of shouty Americans tromp all over. Those Americans, conversely, don't like the idea that they're going to have to build their shiny new Cold War military base on an island with more than 1,000 people living on it. Especially when that island is about ten square miles, and in the middle of, like, absolute bucketloads of sea.

So, the British did what the British do – set about doing horrifying things in the name of international relations. A now infamous correspondence between Foreign Office official Sir Paul Gore-Booth and diplomat Denis Greenhill had the former declare, 'We must surely be very tough about this. The object of the exercise is to get some rocks which will remain ours ... There will be no indigenous population except seagulls.'

Then came the reply, 'Unfortunately, along with the birds go some few Tarzans or Man Fridays whose origins are obscure.'

Such was the British attitude to the local life. The population, slowly but surely, dwindled over the next six or seven years, although 'dwindled' may be the wrong word. 'Dwindled' brings to mind a steady, calm, sedate decline, almost serene. The Chagossians' departure from their home was not serene.

In an article for the Huffington Post in 2013, anthropologist David Vine wrote, 'British agents, with the help of Navy Seabees, quickly rounded up the islanders' pet dogs, gassing and burning them in sealed cargo sheds. They ordered ... the remaining Chagossians on to overcrowded cargo ships. During the deportations, which took place in stages until May 1973, most Chagossians slept in the ship's hold atop guano – bird crap. Prized horses stayed on deck. By the end of the five-day trip, vomit, urine and excrement were everywhere. At least one woman miscarried.

'Arriving in Mauritius and the Seychelles, Chagossians were literally left on the docks. They were homeless, jobless, and had little money, and they received no resettlement assistance. In 1975, the *Washington Post* broke the story in the Western press and found them living in "abject poverty". Most remain deeply impoverished to this day.'

Those who weren't forcibly resettled on ships to Mauritius were lured off the islands by promises of free flights, only to find themselves barred from coming back. Those who left for holidays or to receive more complete medical treatment than they could find on the island were kept from returning. By 1973, the job was done.

Marie Liseby Elysé was one of the Chagossians evicted from the island in 1973, and one of those who gave evidence at The Hague in 2018. She told *The Guardian*, 'In Chagos everyone had a job, his family and his culture. All that we ate was fresh food. Ships which came from Mauritius brought all our goods.

'But one day the administrator told us that we had to leave our island, leave our houses and go away. All persons were unhappy. But we had no choice. They did not give us any reason. Ships which used to bring food stopped coming. We had nothing to eat. No medicine. Nothing at all. We suffered a lot. But then one day, a ship called *Nordvaer* came.

'The administrator told us we had to board the ship, leaving everything, leaving all our personal belongings behind except a few clothes and go. When we boarded the ship, conditions in the hull of the ship were bad. We were like animals and slaves in that ship.

'People were dying of sadness in that ship. And as for me I was four months pregnant at that time. The ship took four days to reach Mauritius. After our arrival, my child was born and died.

'Nobody would like to be uprooted from the island where he was born, to be uprooted like animals. And it's heartbreaking.'

Elysé's family were among scores of families dumped at docks in the Seychelles and Mauritius. With no homes and little in the way of formal education, as well as accents and identification documents which immediately marked them as outsiders, Chagossians found it hard to prosper in their new countries.

Sagren is a Creole word used by the Chagossians. Roughly translated it means 'memory', but it runs deeper than that. Sagren is used to refer to the memory of what was, and was lost. What was, and may never be again. The shock. The sadness.

Sagren. Memory.

Home.

Activist groups formed, and legal challenges were lodged. Margaret Thatcher's Conservative government authorised a compensatory payout of £4m to those displaced to Mauritius, on the condition that those in receipt signed away their right to return to the islands. Handed forms in a language they didn't understand, the Chagossians signed.

Just after the turn of the millennium, a breakthrough came. The British High Court ruled in favour of the Chagossians' right to return to the islands.

Then that ruling was overturned.

So was that one.

The third one? Overturned too.

Time and time and time again, a step forward has been followed by a step and a half back. The government bypassed parliament. The House of Lords accepted an appeal of an appeal. Round and round, bureaucracy continued – and continues – to provide nothing but false starts while the last generations to have been born on the Chagos Islands grow older.

All of this for the British government to get a discount on a nuclear programme 50 years ago.

Not all of the deported Chagossians stayed in Mauritius or the Seychelles, though. A reasonable number, some 3,000, came to the UK in 2003 when they were first awarded British citizenship – the majority of those settling in Crawley, just south of London.

That's where the Chagos Islands football team started, with the Union Chagossiene de Football joining the NF-Board in 2005, producing both a national team and a club side, Chagos Islands FC.

While Chagos Islands FC spent a few years playing in the amateur Crawley and District Football League, the national side did … nothing. The club side won the second division (third tier) of the Crawley and District League in 2008/09, but the competition disbanded just a season later, leaving the club without a league in which to play.

That's when things picked up on the national stage, the UCF attempting to arrange entry into the NF-Board's 2010 VIVA World Cup on the Maltese archipelago. The spirit was willing, but the bank account was unwilling – the team unable to fund their travel and accommodation for the tournament and leaving them matchless for another year.

It wasn't until the end of 2011 that the Chagos Islands made their international debut, welcoming Raetia to Crawley-based

Oakwood FC for a friendly. Raetia, a former (*very* former) province of the Roman Empire and more contemporarily an area taking in parts of modern Italy, Germany, Switzerland, Austria and Lichtenstein, were at that time fellow NF-Board members and have competed in one CONIFA World Football Cup since.

The match finished 6-1 to the Chagos Islands, a successful start and to date their biggest win. A second match followed six months later against the fucking absurd self-proclaimed Principality of Sealand, an offshore platform in the North Sea which has never been inhabited by more than four people since Paddy Roy Bates declared it a nation state in 1975.

The Sealand team featured minor celebrities rather than anyone with a claim to nationality of a platform in the ocean – obviously – with ex-pros Simon Charlton and Dave Gardner popping in for the match in Surrey. *The Sun*'s showbiz editor got a run out, as did British actor Ralf Little, the token 'oh actually, he's surprisingly alright at this isn't he?' entry in celebrity charity games up and down the country.

If there's one overwhelmingly good thing CONIFA have done with their membership criteria, by the way, it's the big sign on the door that says, 'No daft places like Sealand – don't be ridiculous; fuck off and join a circus if you really want to be clowns in front of a bunch of people.'

The game was Sealand's first under the NF-Board, and saw the Chagos Islands run out 3-1 winners. The two teams faced each other again the following year, Sealand evening up the 'series' with a 4-2 win, before a decider at Crawley FC's 6,000-capacity Broadfield Stadium was won on penalties by the 'home' Chagos Islands after a 1-1 draw.

At that point, almost ten years since the UCF had been founded and 18 months after it collapsed to be replaced by the Chagos Football Association, the team had played a total of four games. Then CONIFA came along, and things got just a mite more serious.

A first CONIFA vs CONIFA friendly was held at the end of 2014, Haringey's Coles Park in London playing host to a 1-1 draw between the Chagossians and future World Football Cup hosts Somaliland.

A place in the 2016 World Football Cup was next on the agenda, with the Benedikt Fontana Cup – a three-way tournament against Raetia and another team, which swiftly became a two-legged play-off when the third team pulled out. Then the Chagos Islands team pulled out a week before the tie too, and that was that.

Both Raetia and the Chagos Islands ended up qualifying for the 2016 tournament regardless, the Chagossians warming up for their trip to Abkhazia with a 4-1 spanking at the hands of Panjab in Birmingham.

What followed in Abkhazia was a series of tragic mismatches. The Chagos Islands played the hosts first up and, with their own amateurs up against a mixture of professionals and the best non-pros the large de facto state had to offer, they were pumped, 9-0. The score was 8-0 after just an hour had passed.

A day later, they returned to the Dinamo Stadium in Sukhumi to face Western Armenia and try to claw back some semblance of respectability after the biggest loss in their short history.

Western Armenia striker David Ghandilyan scored six goals by himself. In a row. When his run ended in the 53rd minute, his team-mates took up the slack and fired in another six between them, those shared between five different second-half goalscorers. There were no Chagossian goals in reply, and they were eliminated after two days with a goal difference of -21 (non-football fans: that's bad).

By a quirk of fate, the Chagos Islands' two placement round opponents were teams they'd played in friendlies in England earlier in their 'life' as an international team, a 3-2 defeat to Somaliland in the first of the two setting up an 11th/12th place play-off against Raetia.

An early goal saw the displaced islanders finally get off to a good start in a match, but ill-discipline cost them that lead as the match went on. A well-directed header from a dangerous free kick saw the mid-European side level things up in the first half before a penalty on the hour mark turned the game around entirely.

The final ten minutes of the match were chaos. The players were out on their feet – Chagos Islands had played four games in six days, and Raetia four in five – and the displaced islanders took advantage of those weary legs and their own extra day of rest to score twice in quick succession, the goal to put them into a 3-2 lead celebrated in wild fashion.

The goalkeeper hared up to the other end of the pitch to celebrate with his team-mates, one player did a full-on handspring flip (I can't do that at literally any time of my life; I could down 17 energy drinks, carb-load for days and get a full night's sleep before and not do a flip; I cannot understand how this human man was able to do that, but we're getting off track) and, with two minutes to play, it looked as though the Chagossians would leave with their first competitive win.

It was the 93rd minute when Raetia equalised, a long punt upfield from yet another free kick and a goalmouth scramble. When they won the ensuing penalty shoot-out, Raetia celebrated as if they'd won the tournament itself, leaping on each other's backs and lifting their goalkeeper into the air.

The Chagossians, conversely, sunk to the floor. They'd come within seconds of a win to round off their first international tournament, one which had started in such humbling fashion, only to have it snatched away in the cruellest of fashions.

A chance at redemption came just a couple of months later, at Sutton's Gander Green Lane in south London, for the World Unity Cup – a qualifying tournament for the 2018 edition of the World Football Cup. Victory came immediately, a 3-2 win over Barawa kick-starting the Chagos Islands' competition, before they were bested 5-1 by Tamil Eelam the following day. And then again in the final the day after.

Since then, the Chagos Islands have become something of a go-to team when other British-based sides want a match. Yorkshire played their second match against them, winning 6-0 on home soil, before Barawa returned to avenge their World Unity Cup defeat with a 4-1 win in a pre-World Football Cup friendly.

Chagos Islands didn't make it to the tournament being held in the team's adopted city, but … did, a bit.

When Ellan Vannin pulled out before the placement rounds, CONIFA were desperate for another team to fulfil the Manx side's fixtures and while the first game was too short notice for a Chagossian side to pull themselves together, the second and third were not.

Those games, respectively, were a 1-0 defeat to Matabeleland and a hearty 6-1 walloping from minnows Tuvalu (heh, minnows, like the fish, cos they're from an island collective). Granted the team came together at short notice, but the results aren't promising for the Chagos Islands' team's future as a competitive entity.

They've won just one of their last 15 games, and lost ten of their last 12 (11 of 12 if you're being uncharitable and counting the penalty shoot-out defeat to Raetia). Games against a Surrey XI in Surrey and Cascadia in London will be seen in 2019. Surrey are an unknown quantity, but if Cascadia bring anything like the team that turned heads at London 2018, things could get quite messy.

However, competing is only a small fraction of the point of the Chagossian team, as activist Sabrina Jean has said. 'Our people can't live in the land they represent on the field because the Chagossian people have been exiled from their homeland for more than 40 years,' she said in a 2016 interview, 'but we play to let people all over the world know about our ancestors' motherland.'

Jean is both the coordinator of the Chagos FA and the UK chair of the Chagos Refugees Group, putting her right at the heart of the Chagossian people's struggle for recognition and return to their home. Her goal in the formation of the team was simple: awareness.

The extent to which that's worked can be argued, but the fact that it's worked to *some* extent can't. Those games filling in at London 2018 put the Chagos Islands name into the consciousness of thousands of fans watching the tournament, and of the world's media covering the competition. Small football communities tend to be mildly obsessive about the things they love and the causes that are raised 'in the name of football', and if the Chagossians can glean a measure of public support from that, so much the better.

For all that, the team is yet to secure a sponsor. They don't have a regular place to train. A team without a home, for a people whose home was taken from them – and which continues to be withheld from them.

The ways their homeland is being withheld are numerous. The physical occupation is the most obvious, but the British government has done their best to find as many backup plans as possible. In 2010, for example, they established the Chagos Marine Protected Area around the islands. Like, *way* around the islands: 640,000km² around the islands.

Colin Roberts, director of overseas territories at the Foreign Office at the time, made no secret that the MPA would 'in effect, put paid to resettlement claims of the archipelago's former residents'.

And when I say he made no secret of it, I mean he literally wrote that in a leaked message to the US state department.

The same message, of course, assured the US that there would be no issues with their continued presence there, that the territory was reserved for military uses and, in effect, that the US personnel on Diego Garcia could do whatever the hell they wanted in the Chagos MPA.

The Chagos Marine Protected Area is a No Take Zone, which in theory means that fishing, taking natural materials, dumping, dredging or construction activities are banned, and from which the removal of any resources is also banned.

More than 28 tonnes of fish were caught for personnel on the base in 2010, the year the MPA was established. In 2014, *The Guardian* reported that servicemen on the base – who get their food flown in from overseas – had been allowed to catch somewhere in the region of 50 tonnes of fish for sport.

Sabrina Jean wrote an impassioned defence of the islands' natural preservation in 2013, writing, 'For many years, the Chagossians were the guardians of these beautiful islands in the Indian Ocean. We grew our own food, fished from the sea and enjoyed a way of life that had sustained our ancestors for generations.

'Before our expulsion from the islands in 1968 by the British government, to make way for a US military base, the islands were in pristine condition – far better than they are today.

'The military base set up on Diego Garcia has been responsible for causing significant damage: much of the island's vegetation has been destroyed, large areas of the island have been concreted over, a deep-water harbour for the vast military arsenal has been created, oil spills have seeped into the freshwater reservoirs and the coral base of the islands, while industrial-scale fishing of tuna from the local waters has left stocks depleted.

'Over the last 46 years, many of us have set up what we have continued to hope would be temporary homes in Mauritius and the United Kingdom. Witnessing the destruction of our islands from afar during that time has upset us deeply, as has the refusal by successive British governments to allow us to return to the islands, even just to visit and tend to the graves of our ancestors.'

She continued, 'An independent feasibility study we commissioned supports what we have argued all along, that there is no reason that we should not return; our presence will not endanger the beautiful corals or remaining fish stocks.

'It's for this reason, we find ourselves in the awkward position of having to oppose a Marine Protected Area (MPA), not because we do not want to preserve our islands and the waters around them, but because we know that it is just one of a number of strategies aimed at preventing us from returning to the islands – a hunch which has since been born out through the cables recently revealed by WikiLeaks [which revealed the notes from Colin Roberts, among others].

'We find the suggestion that this is the real reason for the MPA far more compelling than we do the argument that our return would be detrimental to the island, particularly when 1,500 servicemen and 2,000 civilian workers currently live there.'

That view was backed up by a United Nations tribunal in 2015, which accused Britain of acting illegally in setting up the MPA, ignoring or marginalising the rights of Mauritius in order to curry favour with the US – who may have used the island as a black site for the interrogation of terror suspects, in a manner which Colin Powell's former chief of staff referred to as 'nefarious activities'.

'No one has indicated there was a detention site there, not in so many words,' Lawrence Wilkerson told Vice News. 'What they indicated is that interrogations took place there.

'What I heard [from multiple CIA intelligence sources] was more along the lines of using it as a transit location when perhaps other places were full or other places were deemed too dangerous or insecure, or unavailable at the moment. So you might have a case where you simply go in and use a facility at Diego Garcia for a month, or two weeks, or whatever, and you do your nefarious activities there.'

It's hard to think of a worse set of optics for the British government. 'We forcibly deported over a thousand people from their homes and left them on the shores of Mauritius and the Seychelles, mostly alive if they were lucky,' they could say.

'But it's okay. We had a really really good reason. We wanted to rent out the island to the US so they'd give us a discount on a nuclear programme. And look how it's turned out! Good, right? The US look like they've used the island to clandestinely interrogate people (although we're going to continue to deny knowledge of this, so either we're lying to you or we're being lied to [or they're being honest and are completely innocent?]), and thousands of people have been dumped into places where they don't speak the local language and have no housing.

'Also, we're not going to kick the US off after that 50-year lease ends. And we're going to do our best to make sure we systematically fail to support them, and fight tooth and nail to keep them away from their homes, and – given that it's been half a century now – the homes of their ancestors.

'Oh yeah! And if second-generation Chagossians, who we've allowed to have British passports, have their children overseas and then move to the UK with them? Those children aren't getting British citizenship. We're telling, for example, 20-year-old Lorenzo Narainen – who moved to the UK from Mauritius with his second generation Chagossian parents (who hold British passports) when he was 13 – that he's going to be deported in the next year without notice.

'We are cartoon villains who do horrific things to large groups of people, and have done through history, and then attempt to keep up the pretence that we and our colonial brand of evil are in some way not fundamentally damaging to the fabric of dozens of societies around the world. We won't make amends, not meaningful ones at least, and we won't consider even pretending that we've learned any lessons.

'What we'll do instead is appoint as Prime Minister a Home Secretary who boasted that she would "deport first and hear appeals later" as part of a "hostile environment" policy, a policy which included sending vans around to areas with high migrant populations with slogans telling illegal immigrants to "go home or face arrest". Nigel Farage – literal, actual Nigel Farage, the red, gurning face of the rise of far-right neo-fascism in Britain – called those vans "unpleasant".

'Then we'll sweep the Windrush thing under the rug, because … well, you saw what we said about not even pretending to make amends or learn lessons about stuff like this.

'Now, don't you trust us to have your best interests at heart, Chagossians?'

If the tone of the second half of this chapter sounds a mite pessimistic, it's because … ah look, it's just hard to see what more the Chagossian people could *do*. They've taken their cases to all the courts, and won. The government has pulled some legal chicanery to try and get those rulings overturned, and then the Chagossians have won *again*.

They've been vindicated at almost every single step of the process. The Chagos Islands should be inhabited by Chagossian people. But when there are a few thousand of you, scattered and systematically oppressed by your situation, what can you do when the British government – who have decided they own your island and can just rent it out – just refuse to let you go home?

The Chagos Islands need the British government to develop a functioning conscience. They may be waiting some time.

Matabeleland – The People's Darlings

'Zabayaba ya, Matabele; zabayaba ya, Matabele. Zabayaba ya, we will conquer, zabayaba ya, we will conquer.'

IT wasn't hard to figure out when Matabeleland were around in London.

Part of that was the matching tracksuits, part of it was the way there were rarely fewer than five players together at any one time, but most of it was the singing. Matabeleland's chant, accompanied by rhythmic hand clapping, became the unofficial soundtrack of the tournament in much the same way that the team became fast fan favourites before they even touched down in England.

Led by Justin Walley, a wandering football coach from Northamptonshire in England, the World Football Cup's only southern African team touched down in the capital later than many of the teams they were competing against, for practical reasons as much as any other. It wasn't until close enough to the day of the flight that they had the funds to carry off the trip. While CONIFA were able to help out with teams' accommodation through the tournament, getting a 20-odd man squad from Zimbabwe to London will never be cheap. To that end a vast crowdfunding operation was put into action, with backers offering goodies including gaudy replica shirts and now-useless billion dollar bills from the hyperinflation of 2008.

It worked. Perhaps it was a tribute to the growing interest and emotional investment in the idea of CONIFA from football fans, perhaps it was down to the humble underdog narrative, or perhaps it was simply a reflection of the way that social media has brought football hipsterism to new heights, and given causes like Matabeleland's the ability to get off the ground at a moment's notice. Maybe it's all three of those things, and some more besides. The point is, it worked – even if a last-second donation as the team crammed on to a long-distance bus to the airport was the only reason they could stop at a KFC along the way.

Walley was bullish a few months before the tournament kicked off, acknowledging that the tournament could be more or less a crapshoot once it reached its knockout stages.

'I am not saying it because you expect to hear it off a coach but my overall target is for us to win the tournament. I think any team that gets out of our group will have a genuine chance of being world champions.

'Football is a microcosm of life. Good luck and bad luck – fortune if you like – also play a massive part. If we get the money for London. If all the players get visas. If our best players remain fit and free of injury.

'If our best players don't get snapped up by professional Zimbabwean teams before we leave. If the squad is on form. If the opposition isn't firing at 100 per cent. If decisions go our way. If all the ifs fall into place, then there is absolutely no reason why we cannot be crowned champions. I believe our squad, as it is now, is good enough. If.'

Some of the 'ifs' fell into line just days before the tournament. Players were granted visas at the last possible moment. Payments for flights just about made it over the line. By hook or by crook, Matabeleland ended up in London, competing for the 2018 CONIFA World Football Cup.

* * * *

It's hard to understand what the Matabeleland team means, and stands for, without understanding the history of the region. And that means a bit of a dive into the history of Zimbabwe and that … that means this is going to get a bit dark in places.

Matabeleland was formed, as Mthwakazi State, in the 1840s by King Mzilikazi. Everything was basically fine (we can only deep dive into *so* much here), and he later passed control to his son King Lobengula. Then Cecil John Rhodes arrived.

In arguably global history's most common tale, the English fella arrived and things got markedly worse for pretty much everybody else. The first war in Matabeleland was fought in battles largely in 1893, but its roots began a few years earlier when Rhodes's British South Africa Company set up camp in Mashonaland, which became Harare.

The First Chimurenga – or revolutionary struggle – spanned from around 1893 to the October of 1896, at which point the Mthwakazi State collapsed and was subsumed into Mashonaland.

Thus, Rhodesia. As if there's any sign of dangerous self-involvement more blatant than literally naming an entire country after yourself.

The thing about being the region of a conquered land that held out the longest and fought the hardest is that those who had to subdue you will feel a little, shall we say, bitter about it later. If you keep it up, agitating for autonomy more than your neighbours ... well, they say the tallest grass gets cut first. Matabeleland was heavily policed and marginalised because its people were seen as being 'likely troublemakers', and reacted naturally to that – by protesting, and making trouble.

The specifics and more modern issues will come later, but what that early divide in Rhodesia did was to create a power imbalance. People from Mashonaland (Shona people) were brought in to police the Ndebele, creating systematically hierarchised power dynamics – with Shona above Ndebele.

Then in 1980, after years of protests, civil disobedience and guerrilla war, the regime changed. Rhodesia became independent, under the leadership of Robert Mugabe's ZANU-PF (Zimbabwe African National Union – Patriotic Front) party and became ... well, became Zimbabwe. In truth and in name.

I spent well over an hour listening to University of Hertfordshire lecturer Brilliant Mhlanga talk about what happened next, the two of us sat in an alcove near his office with a cup of coffee, feeling planets away from the true horrors he was describing to me.

One of the first things ZANU-PF and Mugabe – notably a party whose ranks were filled with Shona people, not Ndebele – did in power was to create a 14-page document of their plans for dealing with the Matabeleland 'issue'.

Mhlanga explained, 'The first event was the genocide, which started around 1982 – from 1982 up to 1988, to be precise. Most of the activity was very pronounced in 1983 to 1985. I lost relatives there; basically my entire family was wiped out. It is a genocide that deliberately targeted the people from Matabeleland, people who spoke Matabele, and it was a government-sponsored programme which targeted these people.

'But how they sponsored it is that they planned it, by way of coming up with a proper state brigade. They formed a brigade, called the Fifth Brigade, which was sponsored partly by the British government. The British government provided financial support for the formation of that programme, like a development programme; they sponsored the funding and with that funding the government of Zimbabwe hired experts from North Korea who then came and trained these Fifth Brigade people.

'When they were deployed in MB, their expert duty was just to kill. Anything that spoke or looked like Matabele. And they did exactly that. From 1983, the killings were very pronounced, 1984, they were very very pronounced, 1985 still very pronounced, and then they started going down slowly from 1986 onwards. But things didn't end when the majority of the killings stopped in 1988.

'I remember when I was at primary school in the 80s, for example, I was forced to drop out of school from 1982 – around five years old – and only went back to school in 1986. Again, if you look at it, in 1988/89 we still had soldiers in our villages. They were present in our villages, which basically means it's one full decade lost for this region of Matabeleland in terms of the development of the state.'

That last point is key. Not only did the Fifth Brigade and the Mugabe regime kill somewhere in the region of 20,000 people over the course of a handful of years, systematically crippling a 'troublesome tribe', they made a point of continuing the stunting and intimidation of the region beyond that time, into what Mhlanga describes as a 'cultural genocide' after the killings, with little funding for new projects, improved infrastructure, etc. Matabeleland has been left behind.

That continued campaign has long reinforced the idea that the Ndebele people have been forced to accept for some time. Matabeleland is wanted in Zimbabwe – it's rich in natural resources, for a start – but for many, the Ndebele people aren't. That persecution has served to engender an incredible sense of Ndebele people being together, being an entity half a step removed from Zimbabwe as a whole, and most of all being stronger for it.

* * * *

The opening ceremony of CONIFA's World Football Cup was an unusual affair, a long way away from the Pitbull and Shakira-presented affairs FIFA have a habit of putting on to launch their own major tournaments. Instead, CONIFA settled for a parade of teams around Bromley's Hayes Lane stadium, except some teams didn't turn up, or settled for sending a bare handful of representatives, most of them trogging around the outside of the pitch slightly sheepishly.

Then there was a microphone that didn't work, and a load of photographers crowded around a two-person Tibetan song and dance act which, no doubt, absolutely nobody in the stadium could see.

CONIFA does a number of things well. Spectacle is one that it still has to work on.

That's when Matabeleland announced themselves. Midway through the parade of teams, the full squad burst out on to the pitch, fresh from a humbling 6-1 thrashing at the hands of Padania barely an hour before. The defeat didn't seem to bother them, dancing and chanting their way around the 3G pitch while a comparative funeral march continued on ahead and behind them. It feels patronising and painfully clichéd to call the southern African team things like 'vibrant', and 'a splash of colour', but in the encroaching dusk in Bromley, that's exactly what Matabeleland were. Every fan in the stands fell in love instantly. The cult of Matabeleland grew again.

I'd arrived at the opening ceremony with Matabeleland's conquerors from earlier that day, Padania (again, CONIFA scheduling and 'spectacle' is wacky), having had the chance to see Walley's side in action for the first time in Sutton against the Italians.

Three things became immediately obvious.

1. The Matabeleland team could *play*. This was a talented group of players, albeit an almost comically undersized one when matched up against a physically imposing Padania team.
2. I would have had a heart attack if I'd had to coach their goalkeepers or defenders for more than ten minutes at a time. The number of times goalkeeper Notice Dube sprinted out of his box to clear a ball that his defenders were better placed to cover left me having kittens from the press box, and when he chased a Padania forward out to the corner flag for no reason, with defenders covering, and put in a genuinely competent tackle to put the ball behind for a corner, hands were covering eyes. He was still sprinting back to his goal when the set piece was

lobbed over him and headed into an empty net for Padania's sixth goal.

3. The pitch was a problem. It's no exaggeration to say that the team had been training on pitches that a Sunday League team would have turned their noses up at – when Walley wrote his memoir after the tournament, the title *One Football, No Nets* wasn't whimsical. It was the reality of the situation he and the team had faced when preparing for the tournament. Now, in London and still getting their heads in order from a long flight, the team were plonked on to a perfectly smooth artificial surface, the likes of which they'd never seen before. The pace of the pitch was completely different, which led to a host of misjudged passes and missed interceptions. Anyone can play football anywhere, but resources … resources always matter.

Matabeleland did grab one goal in that game, though, late on to make the score 6-1, and treated striker Thabiso Ndlela's strike like they'd just gone ahead in the final. The entire team ran over to a small, vocal group of local fans who had gathered behind one of the goals and celebrated with them, before going back over to them at full time to shake them all by the hand individually – before doing a complete lap of the pitch to thank *every* fan who had come to watch them play.

One of those fans behind the goal, decked out in his brand-new Matabeleland shirt, was Zimbabwe-born Londoner Thomas Perez. The son of Spanish missionaries who met in Matabeleland in the 1970s, Perez – or 'Pez', as he introduced himself, beaming, to anyone who approached him – has a complicated relationship with the country of his birth.

'I moved to London when I was 14,' he explained some months later, arriving at an east London pub on a scooter. 'I didn't really think when I left that I'd be away for so long. I found it very difficult to adapt to London, and I ended up having to make a decision that meant adapting, embracing all of these English cultural attitudes, and almost forgetting my past in Zimbabwe, putting it to one side and saying, "I have to learn to be English."'

I bit back the urge to suggest that his mode of transport, hand in hand with the pearlescent bumbag permanently attached to his waist, suggested that he'd done a pretty good job of it. Sometimes things can go unsaid.

'At 21, I went to SOAS University (School of Oriental and African Studies) to do an African Studies master's, which really reconnected me with Zimbabwe. My thesis was on what would connect young Zimbabweans in London to their country in the future. That process alone got me interested in revisiting my heritage, but it wasn't until November [2017] that I went back to Zimbabwe, back to Matabeleland.

'When I started hearing about this Ndebele football team that was coming to London, it just felt right, I knew I had to be there – and I knew the team was going to struggle to make it to London, so a big part of my year in the lead up to the tournament was publicising the cause and doing what I could to get the team over.'

That work put in behind the scenes, especially with the local Zimbabwean community in London, went down well with the team. Already the most open setup of all the teams at the tournament, they bent over backwards to accommodate one of their own into their adventure, to the point that I turned up to watch the squad train on a rest day only to see Pez filling in at centre-back in an inter-team match to round off the session.

The inclusiveness offered by the Matabeleland squad, whose message was very much one of open arms to the footballing community, has been held up as a shining example of what CONIFA does best: connecting people to culture through football. Perez, for his part, agreed.

'The team has revived my passion for the country as a whole. Not even just Matabeleland, Zimbabwe as a whole. The team brought together people from Matabeleland and other Zimbabweans in the UK, who felt like their country was being represented. They felt proud and connected to it. Maybe not every Zimbabwean felt like that, but I met Zimbabweans who had come to London from Leicester and Southampton for these matches.

'It created this space for feeling proud of our culture, and examining this notion of statehood. I felt, if our notion of statehood is based on all these negative things, the genocide, this economy that's been shit, our politics have been shit … if we can put that aside for a moment and celebrate our culture. Matabele culture is different from Shona culture, but there's a lot of commonality – if we can put it all aside and come together in London, it's an opportunity not even to be Zimbabwean, but just be together and share in each other's commonality.

'It summarises, for me, the importance of accepting that culture can be a much more unifying thing than the nation state. That nation state is such an artificial category and causes so much separation. We should recognise the importance of Matabeleland wanting to be an independent nation state in the current context that they live in, but what CONIFA does so well is allow the cultures in these places to flourish.

'When culture is repressed, people end up being unhappy, and violence comes from that. When culture is allowed to be expressed, commonality can be found, and that's a power that football has. CONIFA does that a lot better than other organisations, certainly better than FIFA.'

As well as Matabeleland found themselves adapting to life in the CONIFA bubble, it took a little longer for things to come together on the pitch. Two days after their opening defeat to Padania, they lost by five goals again – this time 5-0 – to Székely Land, the team of ethnic Hungarians in Romania.

They returned to the scene of that defeat just a day later to face Pacific Islanders Tuvalu in a battle to avoid the group's wooden spoon. Tuvalu entered the game sat just *behind* Matabeleland on goal difference, having been tonked 8-0 by Padania 24 hours previous, leaving both sides with a great deal of pride to fight for, not to mention a first win of the tournament.

In front of one of the busier crowds of the tournament up to that point (and a few people filming a VICE documentary), the two underdogs – sides for whom success meant getting to London in the first place – faced off. Then lost the ball. A lot.

Shylock Ndlovu opened the scoring for Matabeleland halfway through the first half, prompting a choreographed celebration, but the African side were quickly pegged back to 1-1 within a couple of minutes.

While goals flew in, though, a bizarre subplot was unfolding on the Matabeleland bench. Notice Dube, the team's goalkeeper in their opening match, was injured and unavailable to play. His replacement, Thandazani Mdlongwa, had been sent off against Székely Land and was serving a suspension, leaving third-choice Bruce Sithole starting against Tuvalu. With only three goalkeepers travelling to London for the tournament, Walley was forced to name his goalkeeping coach on the bench in the unlikely event that anything happened to Sithole in the match.

Quirky but not unheard of, although goalkeepers are rarely made unavailable with such frequency, except that Matabeleland's goalkeeping coach was Liverpool and Zimbabwe national team legend Bruce Grobbelaar. The 60-year-old Bruce Grobbelaar.

And then Sithole went down clutching his hamstring.

It's hard to overstate Grobbelaar's status in English football. His iconic moment came in a penalty shoot-out in the 1984 European Cup Final, where he pretended to eat the goal netting and wobbled his legs in mock fear to distract Roma's penalty takers in their own stadium. It worked. They missed. Liverpool won.

A key part of a Liverpool side which won six league titles, three FA Cups, three League Cups and that iconic European Cup, Grobbelaar's legacy at Anfield and as one of the English top flight's most decorated goalkeepers has surrounded him with a certain mystique.

So to be standing next to the dugout as a more … mature version of the Liverpool legend rapidly stripped off a tracksuit and began to warm up on the sidelines was a little surreal.

To the disappointment of some members of the crowd, although to Grobbelaar's personal relief, Sithole hobbled back to his goal line ready to push through the pain and see out the 90 minutes. Matabeleland scored a second goal before half-time to retake the lead, and then the green-shirted third-choice stopper went down for a second time.

Grim-faced, Grobbelaar arose once again from his little plexiglass hideout, removing his jacket to reveal a Matabeleland goalkeeper's jersey with the number '96' on the back – a tribute to the 96 Liverpool fans who lost their lives in the Hillsborough disaster, where a failure by police to control overcrowded areas of Hillsborough Stadium saw a disastrous loss of life in the stand behind Grobbelaar's goal in an FA Cup semi-final between Liverpool and Nottingham Forest on 15 April 1989.

The veteran former goalkeeper's sheer presence at the tournament was a minor miracle of serendipity, born of coach Walley emailing him out of the blue to ask for help raising awareness of the team's fundraising cause ahead of the tournament's kick-off.

Not only did he reply to the email, he agreed to meet the lively English coach to discuss what kind of partnership could be formed – only for scheduling conflicts to arise, on account of one of the two men living in Canada and the other in Latvia. So, just as all major sporting pacts are, the deal was sealed in a motorway service station's coffee shop, and Grobbelaar agreed to be a brand ambassador for the Matabeleland national football team.

There was nothing in the original email about a potential coaching role, but an offer was extended and duly accepted – although neither man expected the agreement to lead to a rushed de-tracksuiting on the sidelines of an artificial pitch at Haringey Borough.

With half-time rapidly approaching, Sithole toughed things out until the break, at which point he was poked and prodded by the team's physio until he was in a fit state to see out the rest of the match. Fans of narrative were left disappointed by his miraculous recovery, although those more interested in Matabeleland securing their first ever World Football Cup win were sporting more relieved looks.

The second half passed goalless, if not chanceless, until the excellent Sipho Mlalazi was given the chance to round things off in style from the penalty spot in injury time at the end of the match. He obliged, finishing with aplomb, and setting his team off on their now-customary lap of the pitch to thank the watching fans one by one before grouping up into a huddle for a shared prayer.

The crowd interaction didn't end there, the car park becoming the scene of an impromptu a cappella song and dance party. Fans, players, media and locals all formed into a ring as the team mingled and celebrated their success until the sun went down, and then some.

As Perez, following his team around the tournament, recalled, 'I went to the bar and the Haringey Borough owner ended up leaving us the keys – just the Matabele team and fans; everyone else was gone – and we had a barbecue out there, just singing and eating until about 11 o'clock.

'The same thing happened on the day of the final; loads of Zimbabwean people had come down – Matabeleland weren't playing, but loads of Zimbabweans had come down, and there were parked cars outside Enfield's stadium and people sat out barbecuing. A few of the players came down; there was … no bread, no sauce, just meat on the barbecue. Some random local South Africans turned up and got welcomed in, and that's what I loved – the inclusivity of it. Everyone could talk to everyone. There's something about the Matabele people that, after everything they've gone through, to be as positive as they are that's so infectious.

'The end of that night … there had been a party at the end of the tournament, and I was outside at about 6am with

Justin and the Tuvalu national team just sitting and talking about life. That, more than anything else, really drove home to me how powerful CONIFA is.'

While their early defeats to Padania and Székely Land knocked them out of the 'main' tournament and into the placement rounds, Matabeleland followed up their win over Tuvalu by going unbeaten in 90 minutes in their three remaining games – drawing 0-0 with Kabylia (albeit losing 4-3 on penalties) as Africa's two tournament representatives met, before beating the Chagos Islands and Tamil Eelam to officially end the World Football Cup in 13th place.

Walley left his post as the team's coach shortly after the tournament, although he remains involved with CONIFA, with the Matabele Football Association still searching for his replacement at time of writing.

The lack of a head coach doesn't mean that things are slowing down for the Matabele setup, though – quite the opposite. A women's team was formed in 2018 as Matabeleland strives to keep pace with the fast-moving nature of the international game, while giving as many people a chance to play football in an area where resources are severely limited.

Both the women's and men's teams played a mini tournament in South Africa at the end of 2018, the Human Rights Cup, to mark 70 years since the Universal Declaration of Human Rights. Both Matabele teams somehow conspired to lose their respective finals on penalties, but their presence in regional competitions is an excellent sign for the sustained presence of Matabeleland representation moving forward – coach or no coach.

Having talked earlier about the past with Dr Mhlanga, we also discussed how that affects the present – as Matabeleland still fights for its own prosperity. He said, 'The genocide defined us, as a region. It defined our focus into the future. Our people know that if the government tried to annihilate you, to wipe you off the face of the earth, you cannot expect them to think about you when they are defining state policies.

'Mugabe may not be in power, but the damage has already been done. It is now left to the people of Matabeleland to determine their own future. To expect the people who denied them these opportunities for the last 38 years to turn around and become the messiahs is bad logic. Politics doesn't function that way.

'This so-called removal of Mugabe makes us realise that maybe it wasn't about Mugabe the individual. It was Mugabe the structure. Those who have just taken over the state are the same people who have been running the state for the past 38 years – the man who replaced Mugabe as president was the man who was in charge of the Fifth Brigade. He's the man who was in charge of the programme. He was the enforcer of the programme. The government gave him all the powers to lead this. He was the pacesetter, because he had the latitude to make pronouncements and decisions.

'This is why I argue that the genocide is still upon us. It hasn't ended. The same logic that informed the genocide is the same logic being used to deny Matabeleland development.

'When a snake is going through a process of peeling off its old skin, it may look like the snake is suffering, because the process of peeling is uncomfortable. Because you hate the snake so much, you celebrate seeing it struggling – but it doesn't kill the snake, it rejuvenates it. When the peeling is finished it looks so radiant, but it's still the same venomous snake.

'The guy who has just taken over is a killer. He is the greatest murderer Zimbabwe has ever produced – more murderous than Mugabe, in my view. His deputy is a murderer. The group who have taken over Zimbabwe is a group of murderers who will stop at nothing to get their way. If they can do that just to have things their way, we cannot expect anything from them.'

What the snake metaphor makes abundantly clear is that there are many in Matabeleland who don't see a future for the region within Zimbabwe as a part of the larger state, and calls for independence are growing louder by the month. As a region, they argue, they have nothing connecting them to the larger country of Zimbabwe. They owe nothing. They want, as they had before the arrival of Cecil Rhodes, their own state.

It will be a huge task. Governments in Africa, particularly postcolonial ones, have made it very hard, constitutionally, to even talk of breaking away. The constitution makes it akin to treason to talk of breaking away – but independence campaigners insist that the right to self-determination is an inalienable one.

In many ways, the work to create the state in the minds of the Ndebele people has already been a success. The presence of a Matabeleland team at the World Football Cup is a clear representation of that, showing that they recognise themselves as an entity, even if the state of Zimbabwe doesn't. Yet.

Just before I left Dr Mhlanga, he said, 'Thanks to globalisation, we are all over the world. The conversation is on the internet, it has become a larger discourse. The United Nations has been approached. The African Union has been approached.

'I was one of the people who approached some of the African leaders, including the leaders of South Africa,

Botswana and Swaziland, I was one of the people who approached the leaders of Rwanda and Ethiopia to explain the case of Matabeleland. Those efforts are crystallising into a project which will end in our voices being heard. We have a right to call for a referendum, and when that happens we will have a separate state.'

Padania – Italyish

JUST like in all walks of life, not all CONIFA teams – and their origin stories – are created equal. While a number of teams under the CONIFA umbrella have more traditionally sympathetic backgrounds, displaced refugees, rapidly disappearing countries, etc., Padania are a bit of an odd duck. They're a bit ... well, snobby.

Hailing from the Po Valley area of northern Italy, the Padanians have been a traditional non-FIFA powerhouse. They won all three of the VIVA World Cups they entered before CONIFA came on to the scene, before making the semi-finals at the 2016 World Football Cup in Abkhazia. That semi-final appearance, as it went, was sandwiched between back-to-back wins at the CONIFA European Football Cup. Padania are *good* at football.

The problem – although CONIFA's strict non-politicisation, 'open arms' policy means that they've never been unwelcome within the organisation – is that the concept of Padania as a nation or state was popularised by the Lega Nord.

At that point, things start getting wonky in terms of identity.

A brief overview of the Lega, as they're now called, and their place in the Italian political setup might help for the uninitiated.

The short version is, they bait regional and racial intolerance to push their own, often separatist, agenda. Founded by Umberto Bossi in the early 90s, La Lega hit upon historic divides between northern and southern Italy – divides more stark culturally and economically than many other western European countries – to push for devolution of power and a greater autonomy for the 'prosperous' north from Rome, the 'monstrous thief'.

La Lega are now a major part of a complex coalition government in Italy with the anti-immigration populist Five Star Movement, with leader Matteo Salvini as the country's Deputy Prime Minister. From espousing the view that Rome has been 'the enemy', Salvini has turned the League's sights towards Brussels, the EU, and outside of Italy as a whole in an attempt to widen the party's appeal.

Salvini speaks out against same-sex marriage and Islam, and in favour of Donald Trump. He prides himself on turning away boats full of refugees, operated by non-profit groups. He has taken the Lega from 4 per cent of the national vote to 18 per cent in barely five years. He has called for a 'census' of Roma people in Italy, paving the way for mass deportations of many of the 100,000+ Roma people across the country. 'Unfortunately,' he has said, 'you need to keep Italian Roma in Italy.'

I don't think I like Matteo Salvini very much.

A little peek behind the curtain here – I put off writing this chapter. A lot. Padania's inclusion in CONIFA hits perfectly on the duality at the heart of the organisation, that of the individual and the area. I spent a reasonable amount of time around some Padania players and coaches throughout the tournament, to the point that I rode to the World Football Cup's opening ceremony on their team bus, and everyone I spoke to was pleasant, generous with their time and entirely courteous. It's hard to condemn individuals when you have no evidence at all that they themselves are bad people, or people who do bad things.

But what they represent is, by my moral compass and the moral compasses of the vast majority of the people I know and trust, bad. They represent a movement for statedom, or at least mild to moderate separatism, largely built on a foundation of racism.

Speaking to another football writer in the writing of this chapter, a writer who has followed an amount of CONIFA football reasonably closely, I was told that the presence of a Padania team in the ranks of CONIFA's members, sitting alongside places like Matabeleland and Tibet, was a black mark against the organisation as a whole. Well, he put it in stronger terms than that, but the idea is there – Padania's involvement in CONIFA makes a mockery of the whole effort.

On the other hand, Padania's membership of CONIFA is exactly what the organisation is set up to allow. You can't claim, as their executive committee consistently does, to be apolitical if you start to pass moral judgement on the assumed political views of your members. If Padania were to be excluded, then who next? Do Abkhazia, who hosted the 2016 World Football Cup, get a pass for the ethnic cleansing and human rights violations committed in the name of their territory in the early 90s? Whose past gets whitewashed, and whose doesn't? Does legacy matter, or only the purest present? And, crucially, who decides?

For Padania to be excluded from CONIFA for the prevailing political and racial views of the region would be the very simplest instance of CONIFA taking a political stand. They steadfastly refuse to do that – and thus, Padania must stay. You cannot have one without the other.

The time will come, and it feels as though it's coming sooner rather than later, when CONIFA must choose between its claim of strict apoliticism and taking some kind of moral stand. This self-imposed centrism may have worked perfectly well when it was just a minor 'football republic' away from the chains of FIFA, but the fate of 2018's World Football Cup-winning Karpatalja team must be a turning point – internally, if not yet externally. Standing 'for football' is not enough. Standing for 'free expression' is hollow. CONIFA is an adolescent organisation on the brink of becoming an adult one, and there must be an acceptance in its ranks that value changes are an intrinsic part of that.

Anyway, that's enough navel-gazing for now. Where were we? Oh yes, Padania.

Padania's first game of the 2018 tournament came against Matabeleland, adopted by a number of locals as the hipsters' choice by virtue of their crowdfunding campaign to make it to London and – mostly – the garish team kits they were offering as part of that campaign. A small group of those new fans gathered behind one of the goals at Sutton United's Gander Green Lane … and watched the Italian side put on an absolute clinic in mercilessly, surgically taking apart a lesser team.

The most striking difference between the two teams, as Padania ran out 6-1 winners, was the gaping chasm in size and physicality. Forget the well-trodden racial stereotypes about footballers of African descent being 'big and powerful'; the Italians towered above their opponents. It looked like the most cartoonish physical manifestation of 'men against boys', and cemented the abiding impression of Padania as a team. They were big, they were strong, they were so physically dominant that it would take something special to stop them adding to their European title.

And then they brought in Marius Stankevičius.

Granted, Stankevičius was on the verge of turning 37 when he got his Padania call-up for London. And granted, he's ... well, completely Lithuanian. But he's also a man with eight Serie A campaigns under his belt, and two seasons in the Spanish top flight. He captained the Lithuanian national team multiple times in his 65 international appearances. All told, he played in the top divisions of Spain, Italy, Turkey and Germany. Scarcely, if ever, had a CONIFA team drawn a player with such a CV into their ranks.

How did a long-serving Lithuania international and genuine top-class footballer – legendary Sevilla recruitment guru Monchi personally oversaw his arrival in Andalusia in 2010, espousing his qualities at his unveiling – end up playing for a regional Italian 'national team' at a volunteer-run 'World Football Cup' in London? It started, like the Mille Miglia, in Brescia.

Stankevičius joined the northern Italian club from now-defunct Lithuanian giants Ekranas around the time of his 20th birthday, beginning a love affair with the area which continues to this day. A tall, well-built central defender, he made but a few appearances in his first two seasons at Brescia, but those that he did make saw him feature in a famous 2-0 win over Juventus in the Old Lady's last Serie A winning campaign before the Calciopoli scandal.

That Brescia team featured Italy legends Roberto Baggio and Luca Toni; the former a brilliant forward towards the end of a storied career and the latter a famous battering ram of a striker on the brink of a breakout which came in his following spells at Palermo, Fiorentina and Bayern Munich.

Baggio and Toni moved on, one to retirement and the other to the deep south of the country and Palermo, but Stankevičius stayed. And stayed. And stayed. He played alongside Barcelona hero Pep Guardiola, now manager of Manchester City in the Premier League, at the tail end of his career – and under the management of Carlo Mazzone, the most experienced manager in the history of Serie A, and a man Baggio referred to several times as the best coach he had ever played under.

Relegation to Serie B followed, but it wasn't until the end of his third season in the Italian second division – and well into his international career – that it came time to move on. Move on he did though, all the way to Genoa to play for Sampdoria, a couple of hours down the road from his old stomping ground and very much still in northern Italy.

At the end of a moderately successful first season at the Stadio Luigi Ferraris, which saw him named Lithuanian player of the year for the second consecutive time, Stankevičius became something of a journeyman. He racked up single-season spells with Valencia, Sevilla (where he won the Copa del Rey), Hannover and even Spanish second division side Cordoba, as well as a two-year spell with Lazio which saw him pick up the Italian silverware which had previously eluded him.

All the time he was hopping around Europe, though, he maintained a home in the north of Italy – in Padania, specifically. That, above anything else, is why he became a part of the setup in the summer of 2018, with Padania's manager Marco Gotta explaining, 'CONIFA has no rules about it.

'So we followed the rules of FIFA, which make a player eligible for another nation five years after he arrived there. Marius has been living in Italy for more than 15 years and, even when he was playing abroad, he kept a home here in Italy. He feels as much Padan as other players within our core. We also have other players who are born elsewhere, like [Albanian-born] Ersid Pllumbaj.'

As his career has wound down, two things have been more important to Stankevičius than anything else. Playing football, and playing it in Italy.

Rarely was that clearer than in 2017, when he signed to play for Italian amateur side Crema, later picking up the mantle of club manager. 'I am honoured by all that Italy has given me,' he said upon joining.

'She changed my life, she made me grow as a man. I feel part of this nation because I have lived the most important period of my life here. Obviously, I am very attached and I have a deep respect for my country, Lithuania.'

In the end, Stankevičius's declaration for Padania went all the way back to where it started – in Brescia. Gotta explained in the summer, 'Our captain, Stefano Tignonsini, was at Brescia when Marius arrived. They've been good friends since then. When we were looking for a defender, he simply phoned and in five minutes, Marius accepted the proposal.'

It worked, too. Kind of. For a bit. Going into the semi-finals, the stage at which Padania had crashed out two years previously, Stankevičius had anchored Gotta's team to the best defensive record in the competition and status as bona fide competition favourites.

That opening-day win over Matabeleland was followed up with an even more dominant 8-0 win over group whipping boys Tuvalu, with hat-tricks for Federico Corno and Giulio

Valente. A highly touted Székely Land team fell 3-1 to the all-conquering Italians in the final round of group games, and Panjab were swept aside in the quarters.

Not only did Padania have the best defensive record at that point in the tournament, they were also the only side with a 100 per cent winning record *and* the team who had scored the most goals. When they went ahead in their semi-final against Northern Cyprus, who qualified from their group with a single win and two draws, Riccardo Ravasi's goal was met with a collective shrug. Of course, they were winning. Northern Cyprus equalised but, of course, Nicolò Pavan put Padania ahead again just after the half. The players were following the script to perfection. And then.

With ten minutes to go, Northern Cyprus swung a corner kick into the box. Marco Murriero made a brilliant save from the initial header but could only parry it back into the middle of the box – where Halil Turan reacted first to head the ball home. With drawn CONIFA games going straight to penalties at the end of 90 minutes rather than faffing around with half an hour of extra time, Padania had gone from cruising through to being ten minutes away from facing the lottery of a penalty shoot-out.

And then.

The simplest goal in the world. The run down the left (Turan, again). The cut back into the middle, to the arriving striker. The placed, first-time finish past the despairing goalkeeper. The goalscorer Billy Mehmet wheeling away in delighted celebration, his team-mates and his bench sprinting over to mob him.

Padania, although they wouldn't know it for nearly ten minutes more, were out of the 2018 CONIFA World Football Cup; but not before a red card for midfielder Gianluca

Rolandone for what the official match report somewhat euphemistically calls 'violent play', but could more accurately be described as 'the kind of angry, petulant elbow which immediately puts the viewer in mind of the schoolyard bully failing to get his way, a piece of irredeemably pointless, unprovoked violence which says nothing positive about the man who committed it'.

Acts of on-pitch violence aren't exclusive to players who currently sit in the Padania team's ranks, though. Take Enock Barwuah, for example.

Barwuah stands out in the ranks of former Padania national team players for two main reasons. First, his brother. Barwuah may not be the most storied name in European football, but Balotelli – the adoptive name of Enock's biological brother, Mario – is.

Balotelli has played for a number of Europe's top clubs, including Liverpool, AC Milan, Internazionale (Inter Milan), Manchester City and Marseille. He has scored goals at the European Championship and at the World Cup. He has won Italy's Serie A three times and England's Premier League once. He is, in other words, a big name.

His off-field exploits have elevated him beyond the ranks of many other players in tabloid circles. Once he drove into a women's prison in Milan to 'look around', and at Manchester City he threw darts at a youth team player as part of what was later described as a 'prank'. Again at City, he and his friends set fire to his house by setting off fireworks inside it (notoriously not where fireworks are meant to be set off), before being named Greater Manchester's ambassador for firework safety.

Beyond his boisterous exterior though, there is a seriousness to Balotelli. Few players in the Italian game have been more outspoken about the racism faced by black players in the country, and when he stepped on to the pitch against Spain in Italy's opening match at Euro 2012, he became the first black player to represent the country at any major tournament.

That brings us back to the other reason Barwuah stands out so clearly among the Padania alums. The squad that played at the 2018 World Football Cup featured no black players. Given the political tendencies of the region, he was initially unsure about whether he should affiliate himself with the team when he was linked with them in the build-up to the 2014 World Football Cup. In the event, he joined up and scored three goals in the group stage (including two in a 20-0 defeat of Darfur) and one in the later placement round.

Speaking to Milano Sportiva the following year, he explained, 'It all started with several rumours circulating, mentioning my presence at the CONIFA World Cup in Östersund for the Padania "national" team, a team that I initially imagined connected to a well-known political party.

'Afterwards, I was contacted by some managers of the organisation, who described the total non-political notion of the Padania Football Association, and I agreed to participate with great pleasure.'

Barwuah's absence from later Padania squads wasn't necessarily exceptional given the amateur nature of CONIFA sides, but muttered rumours of ill-feeling and fallings out with Padania higher-ups kept circling among officials I spoke to – mostly second-hand, or 'I think ... but...'

I found Barwuah in a town called Pavia, south of Milan. Or more accurately, I chased him around the internet for nine months trying to corroborate the stories I'd heard about his departure from the Padania team, failed to reach him, and *then* found him in Pavia.

He had just come off a month-long suspension from Italy's amateur Serie D league for a scuffle in a 4-3 defeat to fellow Serie B side Fanfulla when I travelled to Pavia to get his side of the story and, despite a series of emailed pleas in English and a colleague's translated Italian, I wasn't sure if I was going to find him there at all.

Chances are, you've never been to Pavia. Even if you have, the local team's Stadio Pietro Fortunati is far enough out of the way that you've really got to want to be there. Walking down the road from the town centre, vast fields and a grimy river sat either side of me under overcast skies. The closer I got to the stadium, the more strongly I could smell manure. I may be the first person in history whose first afternoon in Italy put them in mind of nowhere other than south Wales.

That manure smell almost grew a little stronger and uncomfortably close when I closed to within a few hundred yards, when the unmistakable crack of gunfire broke the afternoon air and I fully shit my pants with a mixture of surprise, mild terror, more surprise and confusion.

Google Maps hadn't told me that there's a police firing range next door to the Pietro Fortunati. In hindsight, that would've been useful information. I nearly cacked myself and now, from my experience, you don't have to. We've gained something here, I feel.

And then, there it was. The hallowed ground I'd been searching for. My first Italian football stadium, resplendent in cracked, grey walls and crumbling architecture. Packed, heaving with the one entire car in the car park. Which was empty. I don't know if you've ever been to an intact, four-cornered football stadium when it's closed, but you don't normally expect to be able to walk up to the front door. You also don't expect that front door to swing open when you knock on it, revealing a pitch full of perfectly brown grass maybe 20 yards away down the other end of a hallway.

It was a genuinely unnerving experience, doubly so with the by then distant *crack crack ... crack* of gunshots in the background. Someone arrived and told me that I was early – the squad wouldn't turn up for training for another hour yet, and no they didn't know if Enock would be there. No, they didn't know how to check.

One incredibly leisurely cappuccino later, a tiny Pavia squad player pointed me in the direction of the team coach via a laboured Google Translate conversation. As it turned out, my emails *had* been getting through. Ish. Some of them, at least – and he phoned Barwuah, passed me the handset and allowed us to set up a meeting back at the ground the following day. I've never been so close to hugging a grumpy, middle-aged Italian man in my life and may never be again. If I'd nearly shit the only pair of jeans I'd brought with me and *not* got out of it with an interview ... well, sometimes you just stop being able to see the point of it all.

Anyway. Enock.

His brother isn't the only one who's bounced around a few different teams over the course of his playing career, as he told me at the Pietro Fortunati after a training session.

Early in his brother's time at Manchester City, Enock went over to do pre-season training with him and some of his team-mates, although he had a team in Italy at the time. A little arm-twisting from Mario later and he stayed in the country to try to forge a career near his brother – with trials at Stoke and Sunderland, before a spell at Salford City.

Nothing really stuck, so a phone call from Maltese club Qormi FC in the summer of 2013 precipitated a move to a new country – apparently recommended to the Maltese Premier League side by Claudio Chiellini, brother of Juventus and Italy stalwart Giorgio. He lasted three months before requesting that his contract be cancelled because of a lack of playing time.

'In Romania,' he added, 'Dinamo Bucharest [18-time winners of the Romanian league] called me again so I went and had that experience.'

No contract materialised, and back to Italy he went.

Then came Padania, alongside his time bumping around various Serie D clubs. 'The first time Padania were in touch, it was in the paper. In *Gazzetta dello Sport*. I read in the paper, "Padania team looking for brother of Balotelli". I said, "What the fuck? Wow." I didn't know anything about them, but I said "okay", told them to call me, and decided I wanted to have this experience.'

Barwuah talks a lot about 'experiences', and it's not hard to see why when you spend time with him. He's 26 years old, but conveys the sense of childlike enthusiasm in what he does that has made his brother such a cult figure wherever he's gone. He plays football, he laughs, he jokes, he spends most of our time together absolutely demolishing bags of sweets.

When we drive back to town after training, he's cracking up while filming short video clips to post to his 180,000+ Instagram followers, while I sit with my seatbelt very properly done up (I saw how he pulled into the car park earlier, although to be fair it's not him driving at this point), trying to look like someone who fits into this little bubble where things are just … fun. He's spectacularly relaxed. He can basically do what he wants – and what he wants is to have 'experiences'.

'I've been to two tournaments. I went to Sweden, Östersund, and Hungary. Sweden, we came second and in Hungary we won. The first experience was very good, I played well, I think I scored four goals and it was good. It was my first experience of something like this, and I enjoyed it.

'The second time, it was okay. I didn't really enjoy it. There was too much confusion – too many players. If you went there you had to play, so it was a bit of a problem. We went there on a bus, too [note: ten hours if you're lucky]. From Italy to Hungary on a bus ... wow.

'After that I said okay, I'm not doing this any more.'

And that ... was it. For all the hushed whispers, for all the hints of antipathy, it was just a young man who didn't want to take ten-hour coaches to not play as much football as he'd have liked.

'I had like one argument with a coach in Hungary, yeah, but we talked and solved things. The two times I went, I got enjoyment – we went on the bus, but we were all together. It was good, it was good. For us, it was training. When the league ended in the summer, this was like extra training. There was a small thing with the coach, but after we sorted it out.

'Someone said we might have argued because of racism, but no no no. That's not true. Never. The coach never said racist things to me. It was because he wanted me to play the second half of games and I said no, I want to play the first half, because he made lots of changes. I got angry, because "what, are you putting the second team for the second half or what the fuck?" That was the argument. Racist things? No. If this happened, I would kill him.'

He did admit, again, that he had his initial misgivings about the idea of the team – as did those around him – but said, 'Padania is like ... how can I explain? It's like saying "Lombardy", it's just a region. They are not with the Lega Nord. Lega Nord is another thing.

'When I went to play for Padania, people said "ah, a black guy playing for Padania, he is crazy". People would text me, message me on Instagram and Facebook, "Are you crazy? Why do you go to Padania?" So I explained, it's not this. It's not a Lega Nord team, it's a Padania team. I'm never going to go play for a Lega Nord team. Padania is just like ... any region.'

As fondly as he speaks of his time with the team though, Padania don't appear to have any place in Barwuah's future.

'Last season I played for Ciliverghe, nearly at my house in Brescia, before I had the chance to come here. That's the thing with football, you can end up anywhere. In January, I nearly went back to Romania; a Romanian team wanted me, but it didn't happen. This is football. One day you can be nearly at your house, another you can be in Romania, Austria, anywhere.

'Just a few days ago I came back from suspension. It was a stupid thing. Stupid! I only touched the player, but the referee wrote in his report that I pushed him and he went a long way ...

'I went to Rome, to the court of appeal and they said to me "yeah we saw the video, it was stupid" and they took two games off my ban. Now I'm back, I hope it will be good, because now the team is ... not doing so well. We were doing well, and now ... this is football. I believe in my team.'

On that last point, at least, he isn't wrong. I spoke to him in early March, just after a 3-0 defeat to mid-table Sasso

Marconi. Pavia's last win came in mid-November, a full 15 games ago. At best, a relegation play-off is looming, and an automatic drop to a lower division otherwise. No club in the division has been worse in 2019. The team is on its third coach of the season. Enock's nomadic career might have yet another chapter, with a different club's name inscribed on the top, by the summer.

The road map for Padania's next 18 months is much clearer. The summer of 2019 will see them go to Artsakh (also known as Nagorno-Karabakh), a de facto independent region in the territory of Azerbaijan and the hosts of CONIFA's 2019 European Football Cup.

They go to the third biennial European tournament having won both of the previous two editions without losing a single game – indeed, having only conceded five goals in nine games over the course of winning their back-to-back titles.

It would be tempting to call Padania 'the team to watch' in Artsakh, but that might not be true from a pure entertainment standpoint. Much as their well-organised team of Goliaths in London suggested, the Italians won their second European title in Northern Cyprus in 2017 by grinding out results on the back of a dominant defence.

Their trio of group games in 2017 produced just five goals (four in their favour, one against), but it was the semi-final and final where the snoreathon *really* began. A 0-0 draw with then World Football Cup champions Abkhazia saw Padania advance on penalties, and it took a shoot-out to separate the northern Italians from Northern Cyprus in the final after the 90 minutes ended level at 1-1.

They were a bit more fun in London in 2018, barring a 0-0 draw against Székely Land in the third-place play-off, but Padania will continue to be interesting for the narrative aspects rather than attacking, flowing football.

The obvious narrative is, as American commenters would word it, whether fans in Artsakh will see a 'three-peat'. In real English, whether Padania can complete a hat-trick of wins in CONIFA's premier continental competition, especially off the back of having fallen at the semi-final stage of the World Football Cup for the second successive competition.

There will be a spicy subplot though, with a first chance for a cross-Italian encounter with the 2018-formed Sardinia team after both teams were drawn, with the Donetsk People's Republic, in the same group for Artsakh 2019. Padania teams have never been short of a little bit of fight, and the prospect of a local derby is … well, hopefully the referee has a large notebook and enough energy to wave a physio on every 30 seconds.

It could be the start of a brilliant CONIFA rivalry, if both teams turn up with competitive sides. The kind with full-blooded tackles, baying fans, touchline niggle and commentators reproachfully shouting, 'Well, nobody likes to see that kind of thing on the football pitch!'

That, incidentally, is the biggest lie in football. Bigger than 'players don't read the press', more embedded than 'I definitely meant to mishit that shot into the top corner when I was trying to cross it'.

The idea that football fans would rather watch an extra two minutes of sideways passing in midfield rather than some chippy 5ft 7in midfielder squaring up to a massive striker and the rest of their team-mates all piling in five seconds later? That fans would *not* want to spend a minute laughing at a bollock-naked idiot sprinting around leading a train of security guards like a strange, pink, fleshy mother duck with half a dozen neon ducklings? That things that break up the standard, week-to-week action with drama or comedy are somehow bad? Sod off. Give us fun. Give me my naked mother duck. *We want to see this on a football pitch.*

We'll see Padania on a football pitch. Chances are, we'll see them at the 2020 World Football Cup in Somaliland, too. Maybe they'll finally go beyond semi-final heartbreak. You'll see them coming from a mile off, either way.

Tibet – the Forbidden Team

WHERE on earth do you start with Tibet? One of the hottest topics when it comes to international annexation for decades, the Dalai Lama's team, the reason CONIFA struggled desperately to secure a sponsor for 2018's World Football Cup, the home of Mount Everest?

The conventional wisdom in storytelling is to start, they say, from the start. That's not really an option here, delving back through thousands of years of history, so the second-best option will do. Start with the football.

The Tibetan National Football Association (TNFA) was founded in 2001 with the eventual goal of attaining full FIFA membership. That, clearly, is yet to happen, but some steps have been made along the way. For a start … well, a Tibet team exists to be talked about. That wasn't the case in the earliest days of the TNFA.

Putting that first team together was an arduous process. The TNFA was the dream – literally, he was on a cycling trip across Tibet and dreamed the idea one night – of a Dane, Michael Magnus Nybrandt, who admitted later that he had been 'furious' with the Chinese authorities for their treatment of the Tibetan people.

That treatment includes widespread suppression of free speech in Tibetan areas, and further suppression of their religious expression – trying for some time to replace the Dalai Lama with a state-approved alternative.

There have been very few men to hold the title of Dalai Lama, just 14 since Gendun Drup was posthumously recognised as the first. He was born in 1391. The position is as sacred to the followers of Tibetan Buddhism as any and, with the current incarnation now in his 80s, the time will come sooner rather than later when a successor will have to be found.

The Chinese government insisted in 2007 that all high monks, including the Dalai Lama, must be approved by its government. A similar situation, on a marginally smaller scale, played out in 1995 when naming the Panchen Lama, which led to one man being installed by the Chinese government and another by the Dalai Lama, each institution refusing to recognise the other's legitimacy.

The political feuding over the position is a small battleground upon which part of the Tibetan war for expression and autonomy from China is being fought. The 13th Dalai Lama declared Tibet an independent state in 1912 after centuries of semi-autonomy and on-and-off rule from outside the region, and the state functioned independently through both world wars (where it remained neutral) until 1950. That's when China sent the troops in.

Chairman Mao's Communist Party of China, ruling his newly declared People's Republic of China, sent the People's Liberation Army into Tibet in October of that year, securing the surrender of around 5,000 members of the Tibetan army and, the following year, negotiations that led to 'The Seventeen Point Agreement', which put on paper China's sovereignty rule over Tibet.

That document has been fought over – metaphorically and literally – for over half a century now, with Tibetans claiming that the obvious duress their state was under, with occupation by Chinese forces, render it invalid. The agreement, and subsequent subsuming of Tibet into China, was always going to be problematic – Tibet with its lords, monasteries and noble families, and communist China's … well, communism.

It took less than a decade for a Tibetan uprising to come. In 1959, thousands of protesters took to the streets in Lhasa, Tibet's capital, to call for the region's independence. Armed rebels fought and, although the whole uprising took less than two weeks from start to finish, tens of thousands of Tibetans were killed in initial fighting and subsequent reprisals.

The 14th – and current – Dalai Lama fled the country during the uprising, escaping to India, where he and the Tibetan Government in Exile have operated since.

It was in India, where there is now a large Tibetan diaspora community, that the first Tibetan football team began to take shape. A tournament was held in Dehradun, right up in the north of the country, for Tibetan teams to compete – and the cream of the crop were gathered.

The conditions for the team's training sessions before their first game, organised by Nybrandt to be held in Denmark, were subpar. The pitch was a wreck, and about half of it was unusable on account of it literally being a road that people used for road things, like driving cars, walking cows and 'not playing football'. Still, the team trained and readied themselves for their first ever international football match, against Greenland. Such is the nature of diaspora teams and non-FIFA football in general, that a number of players were unable to travel due to a lack of proper travel documents.

That wasn't the only roadblock in the path of the match. Nybrandt, who later created the graphic novel *Dreams in Thin Air* to tell the story of his experience, was outspoken in his support for the Tibetan people in the build-up to the match. If the Chinese government weren't already going to be opposed to the match, and the team's existence, that made it certain.

Chinese officials threatened to cut trade links with both Denmark and Greenland – threatening to boycott the latter's shrimp exports – if the match went ahead, but neither backed down. That firm stand allowed Tibet to lose 4-1 to Greenland on 30 June 2001.

The defeat, though, it almost goes without saying, was a victory. The fact that the team existed, made it to Denmark and played a game of football under their own flag was more than could have been reasonably expected when Nybrandt first dreamed up the side.

'The Forbidden Team', a Danish documentary released in 2003, followed the team all the way from their early training sessions in the mud of Dharamsala to the match in Denmark. It won awards at a handful of film festivals, and ignited an interest in Tibetan football. So, obviously, Tibet basically went five years without playing a match.

The summer of 2006, though, saw an online gambling company sponsor an 'alternative' tournament to the FIFA World Cup being held in Germany that year. Also held in Germany and called the (get ready for the staggering satirical minds at work here) 'FIFI Wild Cup', the competition featured local club St Pauli and future CONIFA members Northern Cyprus, among others.

Tibet were drawn into a group with Gibraltar and St Pauli, and got battered 5-0 and 7-0 in those respective games.

There was no five-year wait for more matches this time, though, as FIFI Wild Cup (seriously, having to type those words again is like driving nails into my prefrontal cortex, except without the potential of the sweet release of death at the end of it) winners Northern Cyprus hosted the 2006 ELF (Equality, Liberty, Fraternity) Cup a few months after their success in Germany.

The tournament was ostensibly for non-FIFA teams, but FIFA members Tajikistan and Kyrgyzstan accepted invites to participate only to have to back down under pressure and send their countries' futsal teams instead.

Tibet were invited and travelled to the tournament, to be placed in a group with the hosts, Tajikistan and Crimea. That group was arguably the more difficult of the two, with Northern Cyprus and Crimea both emerging from it to win their respective semi-finals and face off for the title at the end of the week-long competition, but that was no real comfort for Tibet. A 3-0 defeat to Tajikistan was respectable, while a tight 1-0 loss to Crimea was downright promising – until Northern Cyprus smacked the pants off them in a 10-0 smothering to send the Tibetans home without scoring a single goal in their two trips to Europe in that year. Their aggregate score across the two competitions was 26-0 against them.

Tibetan football fell back into the shadows for the next few years, popping up to lose 13-2 to Padania in 2008, with problems assembling what was essentially a team in exile, located in various parts of India. They returned to Europe in 2013 for the International Tournament of Peoples, Cultures and Tribes, and promptly lost their first two matches 21-0 and 22-0 against Quebec and Provence. As humbling as those results were, though, a beacon of light shone through from the 5th/6th place play-off match. Tibet beat Western Sahara 12-2 to finally record an international win in Europe, 12 years and eight defeats after their formation.

One of the things hanging over the Tibet team is that, throughout its existence, nobody living in Tibet has been able to play for them. The reasoning is simple, and correct: Chinese border control means that anyone who left to play for a Tibet team, something that the Chinese government still strongly opposes, would never be allowed back into the country afterwards. They'd be done.

Of course, this is far from the most brutal example of China suppressing Tibetan expression. Mao's cultural revolution, which started in 1966, saw Tibetan monasteries targeted at a high rate and destroyed. The number of intact monasteries in Tibet went from around 6,000 to perhaps ten. Hundreds of thousands of monks and nuns were imprisoned, dead or had just straight up disappeared.

Mao's death in 1976 prompted the Communist Party to extend a hand to Tibet in order to open lines of trust with the region. After a few years, delegations from the exiled Tibetans were invited to visit Tibet, ostensibly to show those who had been away for decades how much better conditions had become, and how happy the Tibetan population was. What they got instead was a show of thousands of Tibetans greeting the exiles with tears and near hero worship levels of adulation.

That was a bit of a poke in the eye for the Communist Party, who *then* decided to actually go and visit Tibetan areas and find out what the conditions were like (spoiler: they were bad). The early 1980s saw some freedom to practise cultural expression return to Tibet, and an attempt to improve the day-to-day lives of those living in Tibetan areas.

Erm, then there were widespread demonstrations in the late 1980s, to the point that the Chinese government imposed martial law in Tibet in 1989. Conditions have been argued over since then, with China arguing that the lives of Tibetan people have been made significantly better since 1950, with the region's GDP increasing massively since the Chinese army took control of the region. Infrastructure in Tibet has improved massively, and development signifiers like life expectancy and infant mortality rate have both seen positive steps in that time. It's impossible, of course, to know how those metrics would have developed independent of Chinese interference.

While Tibet has developed economically under Chinese control, the same can't be said of the country's cultural development. Local authorities last decade reintroduced what they called 'patriotic re-education', which included, among other things, people in Tibet to take part in criticisms of the Dalai Lama, and write things critical of him.

The Chinese government blamed the Dalai Lama for orchestrating the last major protests in the country in 2008, which saw rioting both in the Tibetan capital of Lhasa and in areas of 'Greater Tibet', in the Gansu, Sichuan and Qinghai provinces, which have large Tibetan communities. He denied responsibility for the unrest, which could more simply be attributed to a desire in the local populace for autonomy and greater freedom of expression.

And so, on freedom of expression, we come back to the football team. The Forbidden Team. The team whose inclusion in the 2018 World Football Cup meant that the event might never have been able to happen.

Awarded one of the tournament's wild card entry spots, Tibet were problematic when it came to securing tournament sponsorship. Not just for their team, for their own efforts in coming to London from their disparate homes in North America, Nepal, Bhutan, India et al., but for the entire tournament.

Tournament director Paul Watson admitted in the lead-up to the tournament that CONIFA had multiple offers of six-figure sponsorship deals from brands, only for each of them to turn around and ask for Tibet's removal from the tournament. The reasoning isn't difficult to see. International brands want to be able to do business with China, one of the biggest economies in the world and one with potential to grow even further. The Chinese government keep a very tight rein on who is and is not allowed to do business in their country. The Chinese government have also made it very clear that they don't approve of the recognition of a Tibetan football team.

The tournament ended up being sponsored by Paddy Power, an Irish bookmaker notorious for deliberately provocative marketing campaigns. For them, the opportunity was perfect: ruffle some feathers by sponsoring a competition that nobody else would touch, take a pop at the FIFA World Cup in the deal, and have absolutely no danger of losing any business with China because … well, Irish bookmakers don't really get much of a look-in in Beijing on account of gambling being illegal in China.

So the tournament went ahead, and Tibet were in it. Success. The Tibetan squad were even granted an audience with the Dalai Lama, who blessed them before their journey to London, telling them, 'Wherever you go, it is very important that you uphold the honour and dignity of Tibet and Tibetan people. Most importantly, carry our values and culture with you as you go.'

Given Tibet's history of adverse results in organised competition, eyebrows were raised when they were drawn into possibly the toughest group in the tournament: with reigning champions Abkhazia, 2016's bronze medalists and European runners-up Northern Cyprus, and eventual tournament winners Karpatalja.

It seemed like some wallopings might be on the cards for the wild card entrants, and those fears were hardly assuaged when Ruslan Akhvlediani put reigning champs Abkhazia 1-0 up within quarter of an hour of the group's opener. Tibet showed a discipline and a steel that hadn't been present in previous European jaunts. Abkhazia did win 3-0, but only 3-0 – and Tibet responded to the opening goal by keeping the favourites out for the next 45 minutes.

Pema Lundhup and Tenzin Loedup both went close to grabbing an unlikely equaliser in the first half, but superior fitness and experience eventually paid off for Abkhazia.

When the second match arrived, over 1,000 people poured into Enfield's Queen Elizabeth II Stadium to see the Tibetans take on Northern Cyprus. Not many of the onlookers were aware that the game was a revisit of a thumping 10-0 defeat 12 years previously, but the fact wasn't lost on certain members of the Tibet setup.

The stage was set for a real 'flag in the sand' moment, as Tibet showed how far their team had come since being torn to shreds in Northern Cyprus in 2006.

Then they went 1-0 down in the first two minutes.

Once again, heads didn't drop, and the team drew together to overcome their slow start. They were under the cosh after the opener but held strong to repel the Northern

Cypriot attacks before finally striking themselves on the verge of half-time.

The ball across the front of the box was a fairly simple one, but Kalsang Topgyal was on hand to slide it home to level the score at 1-1. And then, havoc. The players ran in about three different directions at once. Tibetan flags were waved frantically behind the goal. One Tibetan player – not even Topgyal – broke away from his team-mates to run towards the main stand, slowing to celebrate with a Conor McGregor swagger-walk before raising a fist and kissing the badge on his shirt.

Topgyal had a chance to put his side ahead early in the second half and, in retrospect, it may be for the best that his lobbed effort floated just wide of the target. At least one of his team-mates may have incited a pitch invasion in celebration, or done something obscene, or just ... exploded or something.

In the end though, the Northern Cypriot side's athleticism told. Halil Turan took advantage of a weak piece of goalkeeping to score his second of the match before Ugor Gok sealed the result with 15 minutes to go.

Karpatalja, facing a flagging Tibet side the following day, took advantage of the now trademark slow start to go ahead within two minutes but, unlike the teams who had come before them, made sure to press home their advantage. Tibet did score, Dema Lhundup firing home from outside the box with 20 minutes to go, but the strike was a mere consolation in a 5-1 defeat as Tibet slid into the placement rounds.

Ellan Vannin's withdrawal from the competition meant that Tibet's first scheduled placement game ended up being a friendly against a London Turkish Select XI, assembled on short notice, who ran out 4-0 winners in the more or less meaningless match. Ellan Vannin's withdrawal meant that Tibet were awarded a 3-0 'official' win in the placement bracket, though, setting up a match against Kabylia.

The Kabylian team, if you were curious, represent the Kabylie people of northern Algeria, who were part of the independence struggle against French colonisers in the mid-20th century but swiftly came into conflict with the central government of the country after independence was achieved in the early 1960s.

A great number of Kabylie people have emigrated to France in the last few decades, particularly under the 20-year rule of the increasingly authoritarian Abdelaziz Bouteflika (or at least the people acting on his presumed behalf, with long-term health problems all but incapacitating him for years), who finally announced his intention to step down from power in 2019.

The Kabylia region's most famous 'son' may be Zinedine Zidane, French World Cup winner and two-time manager of Real Madrid, whose parents emigrated from Kabylia before the war of independence in the 1950s.

That's Kabylia. They beat Tibet 8-1, with six of the goals coming in an absolutely brutal second half. Even more astonishing than the result in isolation was the fact that, in Kabylia's five other games in the summer, they scored a total of zero goals. None. 0. Zip. Zilch. No goals in five games; eight in one. What?

Fortunately for Tibet, they had an extra day's rest between the Kabylia pummelling and their final match of the tournament to recover, both mentally and physically.

That final match, against the United Koreans in Japan team (does what it says on the tin really – it's a team of Koreans, northern and southern, who live in Japan but are pushed sideways out of Japanese culture somewhat), saw Tibet take their first lead of the competition. A well-worked, flowing move saw Tenzing Yougyal make it 1-0 midway through the first half, to cheers and applause from fans on the sidelines, decked out in the blue and red sun-stripes of the Tibet kit.

The scoreline remained the same all the way up to the 84th minute, when a UKJ corner was swung in dangerously from the left-hand side and was deflected into the goal by the head of Tibetan defender Tenzin Gelek. The scores were level, he held his head in his hands – and 15 minutes later, Tibet had lost on penalties, blowing their last chance to emerge victorious from a match in London.

The mood wasn't dampened too much by the defeat, though, the players going over to pose for group pictures with fans after congratulating their opponents, and they were applauded off the pitch for their efforts. Despite their failure to win a game, Tibet had taken major strides as a competitive entity in London.

Winning wasn't really the point of coming into the competition – ranked 38th out of 38 ranked CONIFA members at the time they went to London, it wasn't really on the cards. Passang Dorjee, Chairman of the Tibetan National Sports Association, made the case for an alternative goal ahead of the tournament, saying, 'My team's aspiration is to play in the CONIFA World Cup just like the people of other independent countries. We want to show the world that Tibetans can play like other countries can.'

It's very much a case of putting down a stable foundation for the future of Tibetan football as things stand, as Passang added, 'The Tibetan National Sports Association is in the process of strengthening our mentoring and selection process – both at the school and club levels.'

In another interview, he said, 'When we hear our national anthem, and we can see our national flags flying in the ground, it makes us realise we have already achieved a lot. Winning and losing is not important. The important thing is to say that we are here, we Tibetans can also play football, and to show that we have equality.'

While Passang was happy to talk about the political matters surrounding the team, telling a Tibetan activist website, 'Tibetans have no human rights in Tibet and we are refugees in exile, so we are keen to show our rich culture and religion to the world,' others were more hesitant.

Tenzin Nyendak, who plays at the heart of the Tibetan defence, moved to London in 2009. One of two UK-based players in the squad for the World Football Cup, he insisted the team would be backed by Tibetans 'in and outside Tibet' and called the opportunity to play for the national team a privilege, but was reticent when asked by a British newspaper about Tibet's political standing.

'We take it as a sporting event, we don't want to involve football with politics. We came here to play. Playing football and winning the tournament are the only objectives we have.'

The final words, perhaps, should go to Tibet midfielder Gelek Wangchuk. Born in the country whose flag he now plays football under, he fled for India at the age of nine. He left without his sister and his mother, who told him to take the chance to get out and make a life for himself, and his sister. For two months, accompanied by strangers, he travelled across the Himalayas to a settlement of Tibetan refugees and began attending the Tibetan Children's Village school, set up by the Dalai Lama.

It was there, playing with other Tibetan children for fun and without any shoes, that Wangchuk discovered football.

He grew, educated, worked, and kept playing – carving out the life that his mother had intended for him when she urged him over one of the world's most daunting mountain ranges as a mere child.

A scant month before the tournament, he was able to speak to his family for the first time in 17 years. Politics, even Indian society, were all off limits as topics, with a deep mistrust for the security of the Chinese messaging app they used to communicate. 'The government will know.'

It was through that app, speaking to his sister, that he discovered that his mother had passed away since he had left. He hadn't known. Yet when he told his sister that he would be playing for the Tibet national team, she wept tears of joy.

'It is a dream to play for the national team,' he said. 'Football is the game that can make your country proud, whether you win or lose. I feel proud to play for my nation.'

He's earned it.

Yorkshire – Why?

TRULY, the black sheep of the CONIFA family. Of all of CONIFA's denizens, Yorkshire are the ones whose name most frequently draws a bemused 'but … why?' In among all the separatist wars and victims of genocidal dictators, there's this place – a middlingly decent county in the north of England, with no distinct language or history of independence. Not a place whose residents have had to struggle for safety or the right to express themselves, just … a place. Just a place.

It would be easy to 'blame' the growing sentiment of 'Yorkshire first, England second' on the devolution of power and resources in the country to London, with increasing proportions of money, transport projects et al. being devoted to the capital, but there's been a sense of regional pride since long before Westminster started looking more strongly at its own surroundings.

Speaking of looking at the surroundings … Yorkshire is one of the most beautiful natural areas in Europe. Growing up in the valleys in south Wales was an education in landscapes and rolling hills, in bare peaks and green troughs, but the sheer scale of Yorkshire's gorgeousness is breathtaking.

You can head to the top of Pen-y-ghent, the smallest of the Three Peaks, look out and see … nothing. Everything. For miles and miles, fields, creeks, the subtly differing greens and yellows of crops making up a natural patchwork quilt between hedgerows, broken up by the occasional dot of a farmhouse, or a swarm of dots that suggest a little village.

You can head to the coast and see arches, sunsets, natural islands and white cliffs. You can go to York and walk the cobbled streets inside the medieval walls, past the old Gothic cathedral.

They call it God's Own Country.

Sometimes you feel like they have a point.

All of that pride, though, has tended to cross over a little into isolationism, not least in the sporting arena. The plainest example comes not in football, but in cricket. The Yorkshire county side – the only professional sporting team to represent the whole county in both name and spirit – were the last in the English professional game to bend to the idea of having an overseas player. In fact, from 1968 until 1992, when Michael Vaughan (born in Lancashire but educated in Yorkshire) and future India great Sachin Tendulkar joined the club, only those born within the historic county boundaries of Yorkshire were allowed to play for them.

All the while, other teams up and down the country had been paying big bucks to bring on board international stars from around the world – the 'overseas pro' usually being one of the main attractions in any given side or season. Between the dates of their self-imposed isolation, indeed all the way until 2001, Yorkshire didn't win a single County Championship title. A pithy comment about nose-cutting and face-spiting seems apt, but this is The Yorkshire Way:

stubbornness and a cast-iron belief in the strength of the White Rose County.

'The birthplace of football' is a grand title which can and will be argued over for generations to come but Yorkshire holds, if not a solid claim, then at least a reason for a passing mention in dispatches. The oldest Association Football club in the world, Sheffield FC, hails from within the county's borders – founded on 24 October 1857 and still active to this day. Now playing at the Coach and Horses Ground, Sheffield FC are sponsored by a company called Classic Football Shirts (fitting), and play in the eighth tier of the English football pyramid.

In modern times, though, they can only claim to be the third most famous club in Sheffield. Sheffield Wednesday and Sheffield United have competed in the upper reaches of the English football leagues for years now. Wednesday have won the league title four times and the FA Cup three (although neither since the Second World War), while United have won the league title just once and the FA Cup four times – again, never since the war.

Aside from Greater London, it's possible that no region of the country has produced more top-flight teams in England in the past 30 years. Leeds United reached the Champions League semi-finals in 2001 to stake a claim as one of the four best teams in Europe just after the turn of the century before financial mismanagement saw them fall down the leagues and forced to rebuild, while Hull City have made more than one appearance at the top table in the last decade or so.

Barnsley, Bradford, Huddersfield and Middlesbrough have all tasted the riches of the top flight in not-too-distant memory, as have both of the major Sheffield clubs. There are two arguable reasons for Yorkshire's great and continued predominance in English football. One is tradition; after all, they started the whole thing. The other is more practical. Size. Yorkshire – taking into account the ceremonial counties of North Yorkshire, West Yorkshire, South Yorkshire and East Riding of Yorkshire – is fucking massive.

While a lot of the 11,902km² is national park land, the Yorkshire Dales, the Moors, that kinda thing, there's still enough space for the best part of 5,000,000 people to live in the county. Those are the kind of numbers you don't see outside of London, and it's a good part of the reason that Yorkshire has been able to attempt such self-reliance for so long.

But what of the actual Yorkshire team? Was it created as a bold, strong-hearted symbol of a possible future independence movement? Was it a local council idea to bring a bit of hype, *ahem* glamour and media attention to the region? Or was it conceived in a pub in Halifax, aft – pub, it was the pub – the team happened because of a pub conversation.

It may not be the most traditional way for an international football team to come into being, but it might be the most *Yorkshire* way for it to happen. And that, in a nutshell, is the reason for the team's existence; you can say, 'yeah, that's a pretty Yorkshire thing to happen' and people don't look at you like you've just grown a second head.

Phil Hegarty, the dreamer-upper of the YIFA (Yorkshire International Football Association), has admitted that the team doesn't have a great deal in common with its peers within CONIFA; not being stateless, not being displaced, not being de facto self-governing and not with any real pretensions to be.

'No one is claiming Yorkshire is like those places or people,' he insisted. 'But anyone who says this region doesn't have its own culture and identity doesn't understand the place. Which is probably half the problem at Westminster.'

Despite his invocation of Westminster and the implied London-centricity of English politics, Hegarty has insisted that the team, which began as a pub conversation about who would make up a fantasy all-Yorkshire XI, is not a political movement.

'This is purely about grassroots football. But there's no doubt that part of the reason we've generated so much enthusiasm is because people here don't feel the UK – or rather its government – is treating them fairly.

'They don't feel listened to by London and they feel cheated by lack of investment in education, transport, you name it. So, you combine that with this historic identity, and you get this growing call for greater self-determination here. Perhaps we're an expression of that.'

To give an impression of just how the Yorkshire team captured media attention from the very beginning, we actually covered the story of the initial open tryouts in December 2017 at 90min, where I edit day to day. We didn't know it at the time, but the angle we took was pretty closely aligned to the actual origin story of the team – creating a team of uncapped players born in Yorkshire.

Having ruled out the likes of England internationals Kyle Walker, Jamie Vardy, Danny Rose and Fabian Delph (switching nationalities is a ball-ache), the team was made up of Premier League and Championship players who would turn the fledgling team into something genuinely intimidating on the world stage – a team who could challenge Scotland and Northern Ireland in a hypothetical five-way Home Nations tournament.

That being said, it's been more than a year and that starting XI has mustered one international cap (for York-born midfielder Lewis Cook) between them. Still. Levels.

None of those pros signed up for that initial open session, but other players did. A hell of a lot of them too, about 400 emailing in and completely overwhelming a volunteer setup that had been expecting perhaps a tenth of those numbers. It seemed that the idea of a Yorkshire team had struck a chord, and dozens of semi-professional players in England's lower leagues were vying to represent their region.

Official entry into CONIFA followed in January 2018, ahead of a debut match against Ellan Vannin, the Manx 'national team', later that month at the ground of village side Hemsworth Miners Welfare Football Club. A total of 627 fans showed up for Yorkshire's international debut and were treated to a spectacular display of goalkeeping from the White Rose County's Ed Hall, a late-ish call-up to the team (weren't they all?), who picked up his kit for the first time on the morning of the match.

Hall was named man of the match in the 1-1 draw for a number of spectacular saves to keep out a rampant Ellan Vannin side, who at that time were one of the favourites for the summer's World Football Cup in London.

Sharing the headlines with his keeper was Jordan Coduri, who controlled a chipped pass forward to finish beyond Ellan Vannin stopper Dean Kearns for Yorkshire's first ever goal as an international football team. Not a bad one to put on the CV (unless you're going for a high-end accounting job, maybe?).

While the match against Ellan Vannin was a slog from which they were fortunate to emerge with a draw, Yorkshire took their game to a new level in the spring of

2018, with thumping wins (6-0 and 7-2 respectively) over the Chagos Islands and ceremonial World Football Cup 2018 hosts Barawa, a team representing Somali diaspora in London.

For all that, though, it was too late for Yorkshire to take part in that summer's tournament; there simply wasn't time for them to earn the ranking points necessary between formation and competition. They won't be at the 2019 Euros either, with a tight qualification, leaving the 2020 World Football Cup in Somaliland as their first chance to compete for silverware on the international stage.

Yorkshire do have a tournament to come, though – the Atlantic Heritage Cup giving them a chance to settle scores with Jersey on home turf when the islanders come over to compete in a four-way tournament with Ellan Vannin and Kernow in the summer of 2019, the results counting towards qualification for the 2020 competition.

Jersey – or to give them their full name, Parishes of Jersey – were responsible for Yorkshire's first ever defeat as a unified team in their own debut match at St Peter. Jersey dashed out into a 2-0 lead in that match before a late goal from Yorkshire's Seon Ridley made things interesting, but Yorkshire's slow start wasn't necessarily the players' fault.

The match kicked off mid-afternoon on Sunday on the small island between England and France, but the Yorkshire team all had club commitments on the Saturday – leaving them touching down for the match less than an hour before kick-off, a day removed from playing, mostly, a full 90 minutes of football.

That being the case, it's impressive that the game took place at all, never mind the visitors losing by just a single goal after a fightback which threatened to rip Jersey's maiden victory right out of their hands and toss it to one of the island's, erm, roving gangs of feral chickens.

Yes. Roving Gangs of Feral Chickens. Not the title of a black metal band's third album, but a real and actual problem that the citizens of Jersey had to deal with in the summer of 2018. Six separate … broods? Roosts? Clucks? I refuse to look up the word for a collective group of chickens; it's a cluck of chickens now. Anyway, there were six clucks of chickens roaming around the island that summer, causing havoc.

People were being woken up at all hours of the night, gardens were being savaged, drivers were being forced to wait in the middle of the road for – at times – over 100 chickens to stop meandering around, with their beady little eyes and sinister intent. If you've never come up close and personal with a chicken it's hard to describe, but they're basically pure, concentrated feathery malevolence. They look cute and fluffy when they're babies, they taste … well, they taste basically fine, and then you season them and cook them and make wonderful taste experiences happen in your face hole. That is what chickens are good for. Eggs are decent too.

But chickens? Chickens are evil.

And Jersey was home to six marauding gangs of them. In the SUMMER. When people go OUTSIDE. And get confronted by HORDES OF ONE-FOOT HIGH DEVILS.

Apparently, the problem was that too many people in Jersey bought little chicks when they were cute and fluffy and, instead of just wringing their necks and eating them when they stopped looking sweet and started metamorphosing into harbingers of evil, they just … let them go. Then they banded together, because apparently nature is just a nightmare, and went around the island wrecking things without fear of being torn into messy, tasty morsels by foxes because *there aren't any foxes in Jersey.* If you ask me, bad idea. I live in east London; I see foxes trotting down the street some nights and that's *way* better than seeing a lone chicken. You don't go, 'aw, look at the bushy tail' when you see a chicken walking down the street in the middle of the night. You shiver, you push your hands further into your pockets and you walk just that little bit faster. Chickens on the loose are Not Natural.

Anyway, yeah, Yorkshire were knackered and they lost 2-1 to Jersey.

People from Yorkshire have long had a reputation for being dour, and – at the risk of sounding like I'm about to start describing hobbits – being simple folk. Not simple as in simple-minded, but old-fashioned, getting by largely by hard work, penny-pinching and a little canniness.

One of the county's most famous sons, former England cricketer Geoffrey Boycott, became such an icon around the country in no small part *because* he so perfectly encapsulated the platonic ideal of a Yorkshireman. When playing, he placed a higher price on his wicket than perhaps any other batsman in world cricket, always preferring not getting out over actually scoring runs. He was stubborn to a fault, and was on one occasion run out by a member of his own team for scoring slowly and prizing his own score over the needs of the team.

He was captaining the side at the time.

The batsman at the other end was Ian Botham, no stranger to his own brand of stubbornness, who had been sent out after a couple of wickets fell with two simple goals. First, score quickly. Second, get Boycott back in the dressing room. He achieved the second goal after about 20 minutes of play, sprinting to the other end and calling his more senior partner through for an impossible run.

'What have you done, what have you done,' Boycott muttered at the future England skipper.

Botham's alleged, now legendary response? 'I've run you out, you ****.'

It speaks, perhaps, to the wider world's perception of Yorkshire that Boycott became a successful cricket commentator after his retirement, leaning heavily on a bluntness bordering on rudeness which few would accept from a commentator of whom they couldn't simply roll their eyes and say, 'ah, yeah, Yorkshire'.

Boycott is a caricature of the actual average Yorkshireman, though, almost a relic of a bygone era at this point. If you want to see the 'traditional' view of people from Yorkshire, go on YouTube and have a look for Monty Python's Four Yorkshiremen sketch. For a view of people from Yorkshire as they are now ... just talk to a person. They're basically normal, maybe a bit more stubborn.

That stubbornness might be needed if they're to retain their place in CONIFA in the long term, mind you. The organisation is a broad church, but their fundamental tenants for membership don't strictly fit around Yorkshire's realities. They aren't an ethnic minority, they don't have their own language – although some might try to dance around that and claim that there's a distinct Yorkshire dialect (true) which isn't strictly English (less true).

Yorkshire isn't self-governing, nor are its people stateless. But what it does have is its innate sense of, for want of a better phrase, Yorkshireness. A survey in 2014 suggested that slightly more than half of the county's residents identified as people from Yorkshire over identifying as people from England, which raised some eyebrows at CONIFA. Crucially, it raised the General Secretary's eyebrows.

'When we received the application, we were a bit surprised,' Düerkop admitted in an interview in 2018. 'Because we had never heard of Yorkshire. I asked them to justify a bit more what was so special about Yorkshire. And the most surprising and convincing fact was that it is a region with a simple majority of people who identify with Yorkshire more than the UK. This was very surprising to us, but also a strong argument for them being included.

'If we have a political agenda — which we don't — but if we have any, it's that we are basically asking people, "What do you identify with?"

'And if there's a significant amount of people who identify with an entity, then, no matter what political status it has, we give them the platform to represent that entity through international football.'

CONIFA may not have a political agenda, or certainly claims not to, but there is a hint of defiance about the existence of Yorkshire's team. There have been growing calls for devolution of power to the area – essentially, the government allowing a 'united Yorkshire' more autonomy, under the control of an elected mayor. Those calls, so far, have been rejected by the government.

The proposal of a 'One Yorkshire' plan was rejected by Communities Secretary James Brokenshire in early 2019 despite being backed by 18 of the area's 20 local councils, something which a local MP called a 'massive snub', adding, 'The government is basically proposing the balkanisation of Yorkshire and the creation of competing fiefdoms with all the duplication and waste of resources that will bring.'

Brokenshire's reaction to the proposal, insisting that talks would continue in search of a 'localist' approach to devolution in Yorkshire, suggests that the government is wary of the difficulties and dangers inherent in a mayorship in charge of over five million people.

It's not seen that way in Yorkshire. As Hegarty explained in an interview after forming the YIFA, 'It's the condescending nature of British politics towards the regions, this feeling that people, especially working-class people, can't be trusted to make their own decisions.

'There is a real feeling of being fed up with that. People want to start making decisions about what happens where they live, and not have some remote Sir Humphrey Appleby type making decisions for them.

'If you keep breaking these cultural and historical units down again and again, people forget who they are. With all the devolution stuff, [a football team] seemed like a natural step.'

There's a certain familiarity to his words, for those who have strayed within shouting distance of any British news outlet in the second half of the 2010s. 'People want to make their own decisions about what happens where they live, not have some remote type making decisions for them' was more or less the tag line for about half of the Leave campaign in the lead up to 2016's Brexit vote.

While the fact that the number of people who identify as 'more Yorkshire than English' is just a shade over 50 per cent is probably just a coincidence, and has little enough to do with the devolution movement, there are two things to note in the Brexit/One Yorkshire similarities.

First, that the utter shambles of both the Brexit campaign (filled with lies and smears from start to finish) and its execution should provide a template of how *not* to deal with a situation, which is popping up more and more in the last few years, and not just in Britain. Second, that honest dialogue isn't held, or arguments are ignored rather than dealt with; things build up to a breaking point. That's worth avoiding.

Still, teenager Harry Baker, who runs a small YIFA supporters' branch, insisted that things are a lot more moderate than desperate. 'I've heard a lot of people saying this shows the UK is becoming more insular, and that Yorkshire will want to become independent soon. I don't think that's the case at all,' he said in an interview, suggesting instead, 'a regional parliament. Because when you look at the differences in spending, we do feel a bit like we are being left behind.'

On the pitch, at least, Yorkshire are unlikely to get left behind. Unlike a number of the regions playing in CONIFA – take Tuvalu, for example, whose squad is genuinely the best possible from the island nation's population – the Vikings have a massive talent pool of professional players to try to attract as their team becomes more popular and grows in profile. Scouts from multiple professional teams came to the World Football Cup in London to try to unearth a hidden gem, and it's the kind of stage that a hopeful up-and-comer might relish.

The Newbies

WHEN you're creating a large and inclusive club, your membership is liable to grow quickly. CONIFA is no different, with a handful of new teams being added between this book's conception and its delivery. A nightmare for an author of a book on CONIFA teams.

Or rather, a potential nightmare. Fortunately, those new teams included a couple of rather unique opportunities – particularly the Parishes of Jersey side. I'd already seen Cascadia open up their international account down in Sutton, but to see an international side make their bow on home turf? Just an hour away by plane? Impossible to turn down.

Sardinia's induction, meanwhile, provided the perfect Italian cultural counterbalance to Padania. And the expansion of CONIFA to include women's football? Unmissable.

Strap in – it's time for a CONIFA newbies lightning round.

Jersey

Of all of the areas represented in CONIFA, Jersey is among the five easiest to get to for a writer based in London. There aren't any crossings over disputed borders, no Home Office warnings to avoid all non-essential travel – just a quick hop over most of the English Channel and you're there. Brits don't even need a passport to make the trip, which is a deeply unsettling feeling when packing for a flight. (Disclaimer: I threw it in my bag anyway for the sole reason of stopping myself thinking about it.)

Knowing all of that made me feel a little guilty for wussing out and taking a little baby Channel hop rather than trekking out to Matabeleland or Abkhazia, so I booked a 6.50am flight which, it turned out, I needed to arrive at the airport at 2.00am to catch on account of things like 'trains' and 'them not running at 4 o'clock on a Sunday morning'.

If something's worth doing, it's worth doing in the most inconvenient way possible.

The striking thing about Jersey, arriving from the mainland, was the vague background sense of 'otherness'. Functionally, little is different – I can use my contactless debit card on the bus from the airport, the signs with directions are in English, and the menu in McDonald's doesn't have anything fresh or wacky (god bless Croatia and their 'Mighty Mike', and Italy's sticks of cheese).

The differences are in the details. Opening your phone to see an unfamiliar service provider in the corner, shops giving change in 'Jersey pounds' – with bona fide one pound notes – and French street names interspersed with the English. It's England without England, it's France without the culture (or, rather, with different culture). In short, it's roughly what you might picture a small island plonked between the two countries to look like, knowing that it remains part of the British Isles.

It's that otherness, those details, the heritage part English, part French and part something else entirely, that makes

Jersey the perfect candidate to have its own football team, with its own group of people to represent.

UEFA disagree. The European football governing body denied Jersey membership early in 2018, citing a rule change established in 2007 that all new UEFA members must be UN-recognised sovereign nations. While Jersey has its own government and handles the majority of its affairs internally, it still falls short of the UN standard – and thus UEFA's.

The rejection in 2018, combined with the success of the World Football Cup in London and the English FA's refusal to back Jersey's push for UEFA status, led the island to CONIFA's door, and a debut fixture in October of the same year against Yorkshire. That, in turn, led to a sleep deprived and bleary-eyed idiot (me, if you're struggling to keep up) rocking up to St Peter FC on an unseasonably warm October afternoon to watch a bunch of amateurs play, frankly, one of the most exciting games of football I'd seen all year.

Yorkshire themselves were less than a year into life in CONIFA, but had impressed in their early games – drawing on debut in January 2018 against an Ellan Vannin team who were, at that point, tipped to contend in the summer's World Football Cup, before absolutely thrashing the Chagos Islands and London 2018 hosts Barawa 6-0 and 7-2 respectively.

Then Jersey beat them 2-1.

There were about 400 people at St Peter to see captain Jack Boyle become the Parishes of Jersey's first ever goalscorer, firing home in the first half to give his side a slender lead. Calvin Weir doubled Jersey's lead after the break with a well taken goal, but … well, Yorkshire wouldn't be Yorkshire if they couldn't in some way be described as 'nuggety'. Seon Ripley scored his first CONIFA goal with less than ten minutes left on the clock to spark a madcap end to the match, but Euan Van De Vliet held strong in the Jersey goal to hand the visitors their first ever defeat.

Jersey won't be at either of CONIFA's next two major tournaments, though, even if they meet the qualification requirements for the 2020 World Football Cup.

The British Foreign Office advises against all but essential travel to Somaliland, which has been selected as the host of the tournament, and against *all* travel to the majority of Somalia. Manager James Scott said in March 2019, 'If I'm being honest, I was disappointed when it was announced that Somaliland are going to host it.

'CONIFA are aware of our stance. We know they want to develop the game in small regions but the bottom line is we will not be able to take a squad there. I'm not going to go against the Foreign Office and what they suggest. It will be a shame because the World Cup has been our main target.'

There will be football for Jersey, though, having been invited to a number of minor tournaments between other CONIFA teams and some other teams in summer tournaments. What comes beyond is a mystery.

Australian First Nations Mariya

CONIFA's third team in Oceania, and the first on one of the region's larger land masses, the First Nations team represent, simply enough, the indigenous people of Australia.

First things first: it's 'First Nations'. Not 'First Australians', which is often used. The latter term is seen by more than enough people as a forced assimilation into the idea of a culture – and indeed a country – which didn't exist until it was forced upon them by European settlers. If any group were the 'First Australians' it would be those settlers, the first to identify themselves as such.

People get passionate about that. They're right to. Nuances and words matter. Now we've got that little bit of housekeeping done …

First Nations Australians have been failed by the country they now live in. That fact alone is almost undeniable. Between the late 1800s and the 1970s, Australia's 'stolen generation' saw more than 10,000 Aboriginal children forcibly removed from their families and handed to religious missions, where they were essentially trained as servants. It remains one of the country's deepest shames.

Issues persist, too, in modern society. Adam Goodes, named in the AFL (the main league of Australian rules football) Indigenous Team of the Century in 2005, was one of the most high-profile targets of racially aggravated abuse – particularly later in his career, as he continued to speak out about racism and promote indigenous issues.

According to figures in *The Guardian* in 2016, 27 per cent of Australia's prison population is made up of people who identify as Aboriginal or Torres Strait Islanders. For context that's *nine times higher* than the three per cent of the country's general population who identify as such. Fifty-one per cent of children in the welfare system are Aboriginal.

Jonathan Rudin, an advocate for Aboriginal Canadians, has compared the situation in his own country to that of Australia (the statistics for child welfare and prison population are startlingly similar), saying, 'It's the same story. And the reason it's the same story is English settler colonialism works the same way, which is that you find a place with an indigenous population and then you destroy them as a people.'

To call First Nations Australians 'destroyed as a people' would be unfair, though – not on those who moved into their land centuries ago, but on the First Nations people themselves. Are these people without culture? Are they not still proud of their roots? Are those roots not deep, clenched tight like grasping fingers around the country's bedrock?

First Nations Australians haven't been destroyed as a people. That's one of the things Mariya, the First Nations team, represents – a cultural heritage which has stood the test of time, and a place to celebrate and live that. They do that too, beginning all matches with a 'Corroboree', a traditional dance led by a rhythm of 'clapping sticks'.

Mariya are yet to play a game within CONIFA at time of writing, but did have a pair of fixtures – one for the men's team and one for the women's – in a 'Clash of Culture' series in early 2018 against Aotearoa Football sides, representing New Zealand's Maori people.

The Maoris won both games, their women's team beating the First Nations 5-0 and the men's team winning what Radio NZ called 'a typically hard-fought trans-Tasman battle' 3-2, but Keifer Dotta of the First Nations side talked after the game about creating opportunities for Aboriginal youngsters.

Of over a million Australians playing football 'regularly', a portion as small as 0.5–0.6 per cent are Aboriginal. 'When it comes to soccer,' Dotta told Radio NZ, 'there's probably one per cent or less of aboriginals playing soccer. I only know two or three playing in the [Australian top level] A-League. It's very hard for us to get identified for the talents we have.'

There's time to come, and there's work to do for First Nations football. Hell, a *lot* of work to do. But structure, a team recognised more and more on a world stage? It can only help.

On joining CONIFA, Mariya chairman Bernie McLeod told the organisation's website, 'Indigenous footballers have added plenty of excitement and a degree of unpredictability and the "X" factor to this tournament, which makes us deadly! By becoming members of CONIFA, our players look forward to representing our people and culture abroad with pride'.

Kernow

I have a lot of personal memories about Cornwall from my childhood. My grandparents have lived there for most of my life; I spent countless weeks of school holidays kicking around Liskeard. Hell, my first holiday with a girlfriend's family, when I was a teenager, was in St Ives. Point is, I've been to Cornwall a lot.

I'm not sure I can remember seeing anyone play football there. Rugby, yes. Cricket? Some. Surfing? Plenty. Apparently, some of Cornwall's great international sporting success stories have been fencers. But football? No.

For our international readers, or those whose UK geography isn't too hot, Cornwall is a county right down in the south-west of England, that tip riiiight down at the bottom-left of the map underneath Wales. It's astoundingly gorgeous; you could walk for hours across moors, over cliffs, through woods, but that's not enough to be a part of CONIFA. Cornwall – or Kernow, in the Cornish language – is a part of CONIFA because of its history.

Recognised as one of the six Celtic nations (with Wales, Scotland, Ireland, Brittany and the Isle of Man), the United Kingdom has recently started officially recording the number of people who claim Cornish 'national identity' in the census – around 84,000 at last count in 2011, including about 72,000 currently residing in the county.

The Cornish language is undergoing something of a revival too. *These* are the kind of things that flag you up as a team who can make a case to be involved in CONIFA, and Kernow made that case. Successfully.

As such, director of football Andrew Bragg has insisted that all Kernow players must have been born in Cornwall, although he added, 'The staff – including Jason Heaton, manager Phil Lafferty and also Darren Wright, who worked with the Panjab FA until after this year's World Football Cup – are not all Cornish but I didn't see that as an issue … The important thing is the players.'

The Kernow Football Alliance, as the setup is officially known, played their first game as a collective in 2019 against a team from Foxhole Stars, a local Cornish team. Kicking off at Poltair Park in the town of St Austell, Kernow went 3-0 up early in front of a crowd of 186, Harry Clarke of local club Bodmin Town scoring the team's first ever goal.

Things got dicey late on when the Foxhole Stars brought the score back to 3-2, but the CONIFA newbies held on to start their collective life off with a win. Whether they're the best football team in Cornwall – Truro City play in England's National League South, the sixth tier – is up for debate, but they're certainly the most *Cornish* team. When you're reviving a heritage, sometimes that's enough.

Sardinia

At time of writing, Sardinia are fewer than six months into life in CONIFA, and have yet to play a game. By the time you're reading this, they might be the single best team in the organisation.

An Italian region, Sardinia is a *really fucking big* island off the east coast of the Italian mainland, 24,000km² in size (about 925 Tuvalus, if you prefer to look at it that way), directly below Corsica. Which is French. And is also closer to mainland Italy than Sardinia is. Ain't geopolitics wacky?

Like any island in the middle of a whole load of mainland countries, of course, Sardinia's history has been littered with conquests and various changes of 'leadership'. Italian roots can be traced all the way back to the mid-200s BC (if you squint a bit), when the Romans annexed the island from the Carthaginians.

A few centuries of Roman rule followed, before a Vandal invasion (presumably they just graffiti'd the walls and said 'We Were 'Ere', har har har), a Roman re-conquering, then the Byzantine Empire popped in for a while. There was a period of autonomy, the Republic of Pisa came and went, the island was ruled by the Aragonese for a while, then by just Spain in general, Austria were in charge for a full nine years, the House of Savoy had a go, then more general Italian partnership came in ...

You get the point. Sardinia has been through it a bit – and if there's one thing that unites islands who have been passed around like a joint at a house party, it's that their own sense of identity can thrive through that, almost in defiance.

When Italy became a republic after the Second World War, the island was almost immediately given a reasonable amount of autonomy. That came at the cost of Italy deciding that, hey!, they had a big island with a reasonably low population density, how about some military bases? Then some more military bases? And weapons testing?

Separatist and wannabe nationalist groups came in the 70s, with the Barbagia Rossa (linked to the left-wing terror group 'Red Brigades' on the mainland) active in firebombings and shootings between 1978 and 1982. The far-left Sardinian Armed Movement followed in their footsteps, advocating

'Sardinia for the Sardinians', as they bombed and murdered on the island and, later, on the mainland.

Sardinian parties have experienced a swell of popularity since the turn of the century, coinciding with Sardinian finally being formally recognised as a language of the area alongside Italian in 1999, along with a handful of less spoken minority languages on the island.

That groundswell, though, has split the movement somewhat – politically, at least. From just a single regionalist party (the Sardinian Action Party) in eight out of nine Sardinian elections from 1953 up to and including 1989, the number grew to four by 1999 and exploded out to a situation in 2014 where 16 different parties representing Sardinian interests had over 1,000 voters each. Thirteen of those had over 5,000 votes.

Things condensed somewhat when elections were held at the start of 2019, eight Sardinian regionalist parties picking up a collective 28 per cent of the vote – roughly doubling the numbers from two decades before, although down a touch from 2014's 33 per cent.

I bring up the political context not for the sake of hitting a word count (as tempting as it would be), but to give a background to the environment from which a Sardinian 'national' team has arisen – and to explain how it could have a strong enough hold on its players to genuinely change the CONIFA landscape.

'FINS', Federatzione Isport Natzionale Sardu (yeah, the National Sporting Federation of Sardinia, not a hard translation) announced their first squad at the end of February 2019 … sort of. Rather, it's a list of players who have expressed an interest in playing for a Sardinian representative side, but not a list of players whose clubs have released them for the match, scheduled cleverly in the FIFA international break in March.

The list of players is long and, by CONIFA standards, genuinely brilliant. There are five players named who currently play in Italy's Serie A, two for Sampdoria and three who play for the team of Sardinia's capital – Cagliari.

There are six further players from Italy's second division, Serie B, and one playing in the Swiss Super League. Even the lesser lights of the squad largely play in Serie C, while Padania – CONIFA's other Italian-based side – take the vast majority of their squad from the amateur Serie D ranks. There's no way around it, Sardinia's squad is absolutely stacked.

But.

The biggest obstacle in Sardinia's path to CONIFA supremacy is ... the nature of CONIFA. Volunteer-run, not exactly flush with cash, there's no path to any compensation or protection for what are – essentially – incredibly valuable club assets. If Nicola Murru (named in the initial squad) were injured by an amateur player while playing for Sardinia, one of Italy's biggest clubs would be without their first-choice left-back, for whom they paid about €9m.

As a rule, clubs hate that sort of thing. They may very well turn down the request from the Sardinian FA to make him available. That's what happened for that game in March, even the Sardinian clubs turning down requests for their players, citing the 'crucial moment of the season'.

Even so, Sardinia beat the invitational side assembled to face them 7-1, Daniele Bianchi scoring the federation's first ever goal and Francesco Virdis (of USD Latte Dolce, or 'Sweet Milk FC') netting a hat-trick. Swiss Super League striker Robert Acquafresca was named on the bench despite being unavailable through injury, just to be a part of a historic occasion.

He told the federation's website after the match, 'Against Corsica I will be there, because I want to play with this shirt and to represent Sardinia.'

Like Acquafresca, fans will have to sit and wait though. A few months away from the 2019 Euros in Artsakh, a new European superpower might announce themselves.

Women's Football

What's the point of representing smaller nations if you're only going to let half the population play, eh?

CONIFA have stepped up their commitment to women's football substantially as the organisation has grown larger, appointing their first director of women's football early in 2019 with a view to holding a Women's World Football Cup in 2021.

That director is Kelly Lindsey, former US women's national team defender and coach of Afghanistan's women's team since 2016.

Certainly, there are few in the women's game who have the experience of both the absolute top level – playing with the FIFA World Champions at the start of the century – and the much more challenging task of coaching an underfunded and under pressure Afghanistan side, whose existence has been challenged on more than one occasion.

'From the moment I spoke to Paul [Watson, CONIFA's Member Development Director],' she said after her appointment at CONIFA, 'I knew this was a unique group of people, who saw past a "top-down" governing style and were open to being connected to the member associations and working closely on some unique challenges and goals. When we can work directly with our members and be connected to the work at grassroots level, we can build a foundation for success that the teams, coaches, leaders and associations can feel pride in.

'The women's game has so much growth potential – and the game transforms lives. Football builds character and confidence and gives the courage to pave new ways for women. It's an honour to have the ability to build the place and space for more women to be educated through the game for the betterment of their lives as leaders, engaged citizens and change-makers of their unique communities. I look forward to working with CONIFA to build something uniquely special for the women's game.'

A knee injury cut her playing career short at the age of just 23 but never caused her to lose touch with the game, coaching first a college team and then a professional women's team in American domestic football before moving into a more corporate role, not taking another coaching job for seven years.

When she did, like so many jobs on the outskirts of football, it came about by chance and a little bit of strong-arming. Having got to know a number of the Afghanistan team through her various roles with football academies around the world, a little informal fundraising and training help quickly became a much more prominent role as head coach.

She brought in countrywoman Hayley Carter to act as her assistant and, as she told Andy Headspeath for The Set Pieces, 'One thing led to another, now we're all in this together.'

The challenges of trying to keep in contact with teams all around the world, speaking a collection of different languages, are nothing new to Lindsey. Her initial Afghanistan squad, made up as it was with migrants and refugees scattered all around the world, had eight different first languages in it.

A leadership council was created, a little phrasebook was created for training sessions, and challenges were overcome.

That sort of can-do attitude is going to be invaluable in CONIFA, where everyone is a volunteer and communication is nightmarish.

Lindsey looks likely to take that oversight role into her new position in CONIFA, explaining shortly after she was appointed, 'I hope to bring leadership that CONIFA members and women's programmes around the world turn to for knowledge, advocacy and development.

'To build a network of leaders of the game to make progress and develop the best environments for women to succeed on the field and far beyond. I hope we turn heads, inspire dreams and transform opportunities. I aim to ensure we develop the game from uniquely local perspectives, because there are no two teams, countries or associations alike.'

It's not all macro vision and standing up as an example though. 'The cultural, social, economic, physical and mental challenges women face are far beyond the depths of the men's game,' she added. 'Thus, the way we view the development and growth of the sport needs to be pursued on a more micro level.

'No one can just barrel into a country and tell them how to run football; the women's game doesn't work this way. It takes time to understand the barriers and challenges, and then work within them to challenge social norms and develop mindsets. I am a big believer that when the value of the women's game is established, opportunity can grow. It's not a "one-size-fits-all" model.'

The first ever women's game played under the CONIFA banner actually took place before Lindsey's appointment in 2019, Northern Cyprus hosting FA Sapmi at a packed Temmuz Stadium in the capital Kyrenia.

Sapmi is the team representing the Sami people who traditionally lived in northern areas of the countries that are now Finland, Russia, Norway and Sweden. The area, often referred to in English as Lapland (that's right, Santa Claus is eligible to play for Sapmi, and Mrs Claus for their women's team), is home to CONIFA's president and chief reindeer herder Per-Anders Blind, who has never been conclusively proved to own a large workshop full of elves, no matter what the rumours say.

Sapmi's women's team put on a hell of a show in the significantly warmer climes of the Mediterranean, going in at half-time 1-0 thanks to Sigrun Linaker Dybek scoring CONIFA's first ever goal by a woman, before hitting the throttle in the second half to seal a 4-0 win and list what was named the Women's Friendship Cup.

The Future

THE number one event on the horizon for CONIFA is the 2020 World Football Cup. It's the only confirmed event with a defined host apart from the 2019 Euros, and it's set to be the organisation's biggest production to date.

As such, it's probably not great optics for teams to have gone to the press confirming that they'll decline invites if they qualify, more than a year in advance. And so, The Somaliland Issue. It's very CONIFA to hold an international tournament in a self-declared independent state that absolutely no countries recognise as such, but it does throw up a few tricky questions. Is it safe? What do we do if something goes wrong? Is this going to turn into an international incident? How the hell wasn't there a less controversial place to go?

The last question is the easiest to answer. There wasn't a less controversial place to go because the other four regions to declare their interest in hosting the tournament all pulled out at various points, for various reasons. A Cascadia-backed Seattle bid and a United Koreans in Japan-backed Tokyo bid have both been put back to 2022 in order to secure proper funding, a proposal to hold the tournament in Blacktown, Sydney ahead of a possible 2022 FIFA World

Cup backup plan fell through, and that left just Somaliland and Donetsk.

As dicey as the situation in Somaliland is perceived to be, it's more stable than an actual active war zone. Donetsk withdrew their bid at the CONIFA AGM in early 2019 after they were asked more security questions than they could answer (we've all been there with websites we haven't logged into in five years, har har har), leaving the members present to vote on whether to advance Somaliland's bid, in the absence of other options. They voted in favour, and the executive committee firmed up the decision shortly afterwards. Bish, bash and bosh – Somaliland 2020.

Is it safe? That's a harder question. The UK Foreign Office advise against all but essential travel to Hargeisa and Berbera, the two main cities in Somaliland, and against all travel to the rest of Somalia. Obviously that's a pretty significant red flag, but Sascha Düerkop insisted to me after an exploratory trip to check out early preparations that things aren't quite as dicey as that overall assessment looks.

'We did check several foreign offices' advisements and talked to a security adviser to the EU, and to be fair what people are saying isn't that negative. Hargeisa and Berbera are marked orange on the UK Foreign Office's map, which is the same status as capitals like Nairobi or Addis Ababa. It's not horrible. It's a much better rating than any place in Abkhazia, say.

'For unrecognised countries, the problem is if you lose your passport. That's a serious risk, because there will be no diplomatic support. For a lot of these places, that's the main reason they're marked "do not travel" on the maps – if you read the accompanying text it says it's much safer than Somalia, that it's relatively stable and peaceful.

'The German Foreign Office advice is even more positive, it doesn't warn about moving around freely, says there is practically no petty crime and a very very low risk for any terrorist attacks – and just advises to avoid major gatherings and protests.'

That's … well, sort of true. The UK Foreign Office does still advise all British nationals to leave unless they're on essential travel and, while Germany appear to be a little more relaxed about the situation in Somaliland, the UK warn of terrorists continuing to plan 'attacks against westerners' in Somalia *and* Somaliland.

CONIFA isn't closing its eyes to the obvious risks inherent in holding a tournament in Somaliland, which is probably good, on account of … that'd be really stupid. Düerkop and Director of Member Development Paul Watson met the head of Somaliland's central police force when they went over in March 2019 to check out the facilities, and have talked to the police in all of the cities they plan to host matches in.

'We'll have bomb squads checking each stadium, metal detectors at the gates – we'll have a high level of security,' Düerkop said.

'In terms of the hotels, the infrastructure, they already have metal detectors and guards. They're set up. It's not a major concern there. Of course there will be more security than we had in London but it's not enormous, you can still walk around freely.'

Will it be enough to convince teams like Jersey, who have already ruled themselves out of attending the tournament if they qualify? Time will tell, but probably not. Once you've made a statement that strong about the safety of your players and coaching staff, it's very hard to walk it back.

But look, 12 teams went to Abkhazia, where the UK Foreign Office has even stronger warnings. It may mean that fewer western teams go, fewer teams from 'stable' regions who get a little jumpier about security warnings. That's their right. Personal safety is just that – personal. When you're hosting a tournament that includes a whole load of unrecognised and breakaway nations, though, it's hard to avoid situations like this. Practicality versus … well, still practicality but from a different angle.

Somaliland 2020 is happening. So what's that going to look like? First of all, hot as hell – it's an arid desert-like landscape with temperatures between 30 and 40°C from June through August, sometimes even September. The solution to that isn't entirely clear yet, but CONIFA isn't likely to be able to move its tournament to November to accommodate that á la FIFA.

FIFA can do that because they can move heaven and earth to switch league timings around, making all of the necessary players available. CONIFA? Nah. Summer, when players are on their breaks, or not happening.

So aye, it'll be hot. But if you do fancy going out and taking in a little culture, the Laas Geel cave formation outside Hargeisa does have some of the most vivid, oldest cave paintings in the world – only re-found in the last 20 years. They're worth a look.

Just like any CONIFA event, though, the field will be wide open. There's scarcely a hint of who the qualifying teams might be as things stand, but don't expect to see reigning champions Karpatalja come back to defend their title. Your manager going into hiding because he's being accused of high treason can put a dampener on your willingness to keep playing football for the team that he helped form.

Beyond that, you can expect to see some old favourites, Northern Cyprus, Padania, Abkhazia et al. on the list of qualifiers. There'll be a few wild cards; Kabylia might make it back for their 'nothing nothing nothing EVERYTHING nothing' style of attacking play, and then there are the new members.

Those new members aren't just teams like Sardinia and Jersey, who joined since the last tournament, but possibly members yet to arrive in the CONIFA ranks.

The organisation has stopped actively looking for new teams, but members and fans continue to encourage others to apply. One team who could be joining the ranks, although not in time for Somaliland, is Catalunya.

The Catalan team is one of the most established non-FIFA 'national' sides, playing their first game (against France) over a century ago and popping up semi-regularly since. Eighteen games in 22 years from 1912 to 1934 implied a certain appetite for the side, but the Spanish Civil War and Franco's rule changed that entirely.

Dictators don't love fringe elements. Barcelona's club team, one of the great Spanish sides, were victims of a cultural suppression – being forced to change their name from the Catalan styling of Futbol Club Barcelona to the Castilian Club de Fútbol Barcelona and remove the Catalan flag from their badge, among other things.

Between the outbreak of the Civil War in 1939 and Franco's death at the end of 1975, Catalunya played a total of three matches. Two of them were against a Spanish national team, the first resulting in a 3-1 win and the second (six years later) a 6-0 revenge win.

The team didn't really get back on its feet until the 1990s, but has scarcely gone more than a year without a match since it returned with a 1-1 draw with Bulgaria in La Liga's 1997 winter break, Dani Garcia scoring the first Catalan goal in over 20 years.

With a mixture of games being played in summer and winter league breaks, and some 'guest' stars like Hristo Stoichkov and, for one game after Franco's death, Dutch Barcelona stars Johan Neeskens and Johan Cruyff, Catalunya felt a bit like an exhibition team rather than a fully fledged side.

The team which came together in 2019 for a friendly against Venezuela, though? That felt deadly serious. Some players weren't released for the game by their clubs, but the Catalan trio of Barça, Girona and Espanyol provided nine players (including future Barça president Gerard Pique), and just three of the 20 men play outside of their current country's top flight. They're a Proper Force.

The Catalan nationalism conversation is one of the most prominent in Europe this decade, with football linked unusually closely to that cause. Under Franco, the narrative became the Spanish establishment, represented by Real Madrid, versus Barcelona and 'freedom', and that has persisted to an extent.

Barcelona defender Oleguer was shortlisted for the Spain national team squad in 2005, and rejected the call-up. He played six times for Catalunya, and released a book during his career (*Camí d'Itaca*) which showcased his left-wing, pro-independence views – but not too many associate the Catalan 'national' side so strongly with … well, anything.

Speaking to a Catalan friend the week before the match, she called the team 'largely symbolic'. The main concern wasn't whether they won a friendly or lost it – their first in two and a half years, the longest gap in two decades – but whether Barcelona lynchpin Gerard Pique got injured.

It was shortly before the previous match, a 3-3 draw against Tunisia, that CONIFA were in talks with the Catalan organisers about possible membership. A flight was delayed, a meeting missed and never rearranged, and an opportunity gone.

Sardinia's presence could reopen the door, though – their FA 'closely in touch' with Catalunya's. Catalunya aren't the only possible members Sardinia could help bring in, though; they're facing off against Corsica in their next match, another team who play FIFA members from time to time.

If Catalunya become members of CONIFA and go to a major tournament with anything like a full-strength squad, they will win it. There is absolutely no doubt about that. Catalunyan centre-back Gerard Pique has won the Spanish league (seven times), the Champions League (four times), the Spanish Cup and Super Cup six times apiece, the World Cup and the European Championship. He has won FIFA's Club World Cup three times. Gerard Pique wins things. Absolutely relentlessly.

Pique could anchor a team to CONIFA relevance even without quality around him, but the presences of Marc Bartra, Aleix Vidal, Bojan Krkic (shut up Premier League fans, he's still better than 90 per cent of the footballers in the country), Oriol Romeu and … look, Catalunya would eat CONIFA tournaments for breakfast if they joined and put out a full-strength side.

You even could make a very strong argument that Lionel Messi, possibly the single best footballer of all time, could qualify for Catalunya on residency grounds. He moved to the area at the age of 13 and never left. Just imagine.

He might even be justified in doing so, for competitive reasons. The single knock against his Greatest Of All

Time status is his lack of trophies on the international stage, hamstrung by an Argentina side packed with barely competent defenders and strikers who disappear on a yearly basis only to be replaced by identical lookalikes who have never heard of football.

The week before Catalunya played Venezuela in 2019, Argentina – with Messi pulling the strings – faced off against the same opponent. Messi was brilliant, and created heaps of chances which were missed by his team-mates. Argentina lost 3-1. Four days later, Catalunya were celebrating a 2-1 win over the South American side.

Of course, practicality will interfere. Barcelona would have a fit if Messi and Pique played six games in ten days without payment or insurance at the end of a busy season. Catalunya may not ever even join CONIFA. But it's fun to dream, isn't it?

'Growth is always good, and something that probably needs to happen in the long run.'

That's the line I've been given when it comes to the ongoing expansion of CONIFA membership. Growth is good, although it's not actively being sought.

'The big challenge that comes with it is hosting tournaments.'

The frustration is evident in Düerkop's voice. 'Just one World Cup every other year isn't enough. Most of the members will sit around being bored most of the time, and that's becoming our main challenge. There aren't too many places left who can hold the tournaments with the aid of governmental backing like Somaliland is now doing and Abkhazia did.

'We're running out of places like that, which have the infrastructure and the will to do it. London was amazing, but it was still a financial loss for us. Maybe every four years we'll have to fall back and do that, but it's hard.

'The same is even more true of smaller tournaments. Our Asia president has been running around in circles for three years now and is struggling to find anyone keen to host an Asian Cup. They need an Asian Cup and the teams want to play in one, but none of the teams want to host.'

Unless a government wants to take up the cost of hosting to benefit their region, as with Abkhazia and Somaliland, international football tournaments are expensive. Players have to be accommodated (12 squads of 23 plus staff? That's a good 300 beds for a fortnight, for a start) and fed, stadiums and grounds have to be rented, security has to be handled, and that's before you start getting into publicising the thing.

Corporate sponsorship, as CONIFA found ahead of London 2018, is a nightmare when you're dealing with delicately poised political situations. Most brands err on the side of safety when they're putting their names on things, and 'safety' isn't usually represented by a European competition held in a self-declared independent region that has invited teams from at least two active war zones to compete in it. So money? Money is hard.

I've mentioned safety already, and now I'm going to do it again. Safety. Unrecognised regions may have all the infrastructure on a domestic level, and life for citizens may go along entirely as it would anywhere else – but that doesn't mean they've got any embassies there for when things go wrong for foreign visitors. Have your passport taken off you in Artsakh and be kidnapped, who helps? Is it the British embassy in Armenia? After all, the president of Armenia called Artsakh 'an inseparable part of Armenia' in 2015.

On the other hand, Artsakh *is* internationally recognised as being a region of Azerbaijan. So is it the British embassy in Baku who come in? Someone's going to get pissed off, either way. Suddenly, you've got an international incident on your hands. All of this is hypothetical, of course, but it illustrates the tightrope that CONIFA has to walk between throwing the tournament to any old region and its responsibility to ensure the safety of its travelling members.

So if there's a safe place which has managed to secure the funding necessary to host the tournament, all you have to do is make sure that they don't have any outstanding tensions with teams you'd like to invite. Then organise a whole tournament. *And* hope it all goes well.

Hell, London 2018 was generally considered a successful tournament and it ended with one team provisionally kicked out of the organisation and another banned from *an entire country*. Their manager is in hiding because he's wanted on suspicion of *high treason against an actual country*. The fucking president of Hungary is *personally involved*. AND THIS WAS A SUCCESSFUL TOURNAMENT IN LONDON. ENGLAND. WHERE MATTERS ARE BASICALLY STABLE EXCEPT FOR THE BREXIT THING.

Oh, and while we're speaking about politics … CONIFA has to deal with its own at some point. My overwhelming feeling is that it isn't going to happen. Executive committee members delivering quotes like this don't help that.

'The whole wording of non-political … for us, it was never the main word we stand for. What we stand for is to keep our politics off the pitch, which is absolutely necessary. You can't get Nagorno-Karabakh, Western Armenia, Kurdistan and Northern Cyprus in one organisation if you let people talk about daily politics during a meeting or in a match.

'On the other hand, if the Turkish government wanted to put in half a million in aid for the World Football Cup in Somaliland, we wouldn't turn it down.'

The last example given there is one that brushes lightly against an accusation levelled against CONIFA as the organisation has grown. There are a lot of Russian-backed 'states' in the membership, and in the current climate – Putin, Brexit, US elections, you know the rest – that sort of thing tends to raise eyebrows.

The 2019 Euros aren't being hosted in a Russian-backed region, but four of the 12 teams entered rely on military or financial support from the superpower (Donetsk, Luhansk, Abkhazia and South Ossetia). Donetsk and Luhansk were covered in relation to Karpatalja earlier, while South Ossetia and Abkhazia are both breakaway states 'in' Georgia.

CONIFA have actually reached out to the Russian state in the past with a view to getting the Russian government to fund a football development project in Nauru, given their status as one of the world's leading providers of development aid – even if some of that aid comes with strings attached.

There was no response. In fact, the only time Russian officials have really been involved in CONIFA's business was when a potential Chechnya team was mooted, only for a meeting about developing the setup to be nixed. By Moscow. Despite admitting that they'd be open to being involved in football development projects funded by Moscow, one official dryly told me, 'We can't say we've had a lot of support from Russia so far.'

So, why so many post-Soviet, Russian-backed de facto nations in CONIFA? Erm, because a lot of the biggest de facto nations are … post-Soviet and Russian-backed. As much as a little bit of Cold War intrigue would probably make for a brilliant late twist in a book, there's just no hard evidence for it beyond the circumstantial. If the core idea of CONIFA was to fill in the spaces on the map where football doesn't go, they've done that – both with areas like Western Sahara and Somaliland and with Abkhazia, Donetsk et al.

Of course, the continual recognition of these states brings things all the way back around to the question underlying CONIFA's off-field activities. What *is* too political? The EU have had some discussions behind closed doors with a view to financing a football league in South Ossetia. The stated intention is good.

The outcome, too, likely good. But development projects in diplomatically unstable zones are hard to take at face value without looking at the motivation behind them; and it's not hard to see why the EU would be keen to develop a foothold in these places.

CONIFA General Secretary Düerkop does development work for the German government himself and, despite every development project establishing in its contract very early on that it's a non-political arrangement, he admits, 'There might be implication. In Somaliland, people were in love with Germany, because the German government does great development projects there. It has an influence on people there, so maybe you can see it as a political thing.'

To call CONIFA a political pawn would be equal parts patronising and untrue, but there does seem to be an unwillingness to consider the wider political consequences of their actions. To boil down what I've taken from a year of talking to people in CONIFA to something pithy and oversimplified: funding football in their members' areas? Good. Other things that happen because of that, like arrests and rising nationalist/independence movements? Not their responsibility. This is just about allowing expression, and what people do with that expression is up to them.

'I think one "political" aim we probably have is to get the controversy running,' Düerkop told me early in 2019. 'By having a Padania team, people start to talk about the idea of Padania and then they make up their mind. If they come to the idea that it's bollocks and shouldn't exist then fine, but at least they've thought about it.

'Take Yorkshire. I never realised they thought they had their own identity or were different to any other part of the UK. It's completely unheard outside the UK, but now people recognise it and can start to debate it.

'And that's good.'

Extra Time

Double International

Not content with having a former Lithuania captain and two Olympic sprinters at the London 2018 tournament, CONIFA also welcomed the presence of the first man to play in a FIFA World Cup and a CONIFA World Football Cup.

Step onto the stage, An Yong-Hak.

An is a Zainichi Korean – a person of Korean heritage born and raised in Japan, often somewhat marginalised by Japanese society. A veteran of three FIFA World Cup qualifying campaigns and the actual, proper, FIFA World Cup itself in South Africa in 2010, he had comfortably the most international pedigree of any player at the CONIFA World Football Cup when he agreed to take the pitch for the United Koreans in Japan team.

His tournament ended abruptly on the second matchday, falling heavily in a 0-0 draw against Kabylia (I was there, and if I'd been accompanied by a Guinness observer we might've been able to write about a new world record for offsides in a single game) and leaving the game with an ice pack on a broken arm. That was the bad news. The good news, though, was that the 39-year-old K-League winner still had a large part to play in the team's fortunes for the rest of the tournament. Not only was he in London to play an anchoring defensive role in the team, he was also the team's manager.

One of somewhere between 750,000 and 1,000,000 ethnic Koreans living in Japan, An has never lived in North Korea – the country he represented at FIFA's World Cup in South Africa. His grandparents moved to Japan from the Korean Peninsula before the country was split (whether that was by choice is ambiguous – Japan annexed the peninsula in 1910 and did, in the Second World War, bring some Koreans to work in the country against their will), and his mother and father were both born and raised in Japan.

Ordinarily by the third generation of an immigrant family, there's an element of naturalisation. Integrating into schools, getting passports, voting, all that jazz. For Zainichi (the word literally means 'staying in Japan') Koreans, that isn't the case. With dual citizenship not an option thanks to the Japanese government, only around 10,000 Zainichi Koreans naturalise each year, and the rest generally travel on Korean passports. Which Korea, though, is often the tricky question.

Because Zainichi Koreans (or their forebears, at least) moved to Japan before Korea was split in 1948, their nationality – simply Korean, not Northern or Southern – doesn't exist. Some Koreans from the North refer to themselves as 'Chosun', the Korean name for Korean before the country was divided.

The process of Korean citizenship, looking from the outside, seems a little arbitrary, although An told *The Guardian* in 2008, 'I went to a school that follows the North Korean education system. I received a passport from the

North. My life is deeply connected to the history of the Korean Peninsula.'

That Korean citizenship makes life difficult for FC Korea, though, a pan-Korean team founded in the 1960s as 'Zainichi Chosen Football Club'. They play in a regional league in Japan now and, despite a stated intention to become a professional team in the J-League (Japan's national league structure), they have a problem. J-League clubs are allowed a maximum of five foreign players in their squad and, despite being born and raised in Japan, Zainichi Koreans can't play on Korean passports. They count as foreign. There *can't* be a Korean J-League team.

And so, United Koreans in Japan. With FC Korea hitting something of a ceiling, the next step was international – Japanese journalist Motoko Jitsukwa floating the idea after covering the inaugural CONIFA World Football Cup in 2014.

A strong case for membership to CONIFA was presented and accepted, and the team (without An at the time) finished seventh out of 12 teams at the 2016 World Football Cup in Abkhazia.

The citizenship thing continues to be weird as all hell. UKJ's captain in London, Son Min-cheol, has played in both India and Thailand, and considers himself a Japanese-born North Korean. He switched his passport from North to South Korean a few years ago to make it easier to travel around the world and play for different clubs, and … honestly, I've looked into it and I think I just don't understand the laws of devolved states enough to get it. I've asked Motoko to explain it to me as if I'm an idiot, I've Googled for hours and got lost down all sorts of rabbit holes and I *think* I kind of understand how it's possible to just up and decide your nationality is different to what it was yesterday for the sake of bureaucracy, but I'm not sure and I'm *definitely* not certain enough to put it in writing.

Let it be enough that it's possible.

Son was recruited to the UKJ team by An himself, who phoned around Zainichi Koreans he knew when he was putting his squad together.

Just eight years before assembling a squad himself to take to London, all of whom lived in Japan, An was preparing for an entirely different World Cup and – born and living in Japan – it was a completely different experience. He used to only visit North Korea when summoned irregularly for international duty, heading to Pyongyang to train. He assembled one squad by phone, but wasn't even able to call the North Korean residents he played with for the DPRK.

That part of the myth is true. The lie, and an oft-repeated one, was that the North Korean players and staff were heavily punished after returning from South Africa with three defeats from three games – a respectable 2-1 defeat to Brazil followed up by a 7-0 hammering by Portugal and a 3-0 loss to the Ivory Coast.

There were murmurings of work camps, mines and beatings, easy to spread with an obvious Western willingness to believe outlandish stories about the regime in Pyongyang. Many of the outlandish, brutal stories are true. This one isn't.

As An is keen to point out (and the look on his face as the question is translated suggests he's been asked the question more than enough times), the goalkeeper from all three of that summer's defeats didn't just keep his place for a handful more games and fall away in disgrace – he's won the country's 'best player' award multiple times since. He is the nation's all-time leading appearance maker. He is, in short, not someone who was put to hard work in mines as a punishment for letting some goals in.

An's 2018 team fare much better at the back than his 2010 side, even if he's unable to take part beyond their second game. The side, containing a school football coach, staff of Korean restaurants, teachers, and university students, kept two clean sheets in their first two games – drawing both 0-0 before their final group match against Panjab. Mun Su-hyeon was the hero in the 94th minute at Slough's Arbour Park, but his 25-yard thunderbolt was only enough to snatch a point after an early penalty for Panjab.

Three draws wasn't enough for a spot in the quarter-finals, dropping UKJ into the placement rounds. A 5-0 hammering of Tuvalu followed, before defeat to reigning champions (for a few more days) Abkhazia and a dramatic final-day penalty shoot-out win over Tibet.

Only the two finalists lost fewer games inside 90 minutes than UKJ's one, leaving their 11th place out of 16 looking a little unjust. Their overall goal difference of +3 compared favourably, say, to eighth-placed Barawa's -15.

Expect to see the passionate, united Koreans in 2020 – although even a healed arm is unlikely to tempt An to play one last time at the age of 41. Two World Cups is enough.

Abkhazia – Champions, Defeated

As brilliant as the spectacle was in London when Karpatalja were crowned CONIFA world champions, the scenes in Abkhazia two years earlier were something else entirely. Ten thousand people packed into a 5,000-capacity stadium between the Black Sea and the Greater Caucasus mountains. Flashing lights and pyrotechnics. A pitch invasion. A de facto state's government present, partisan, cheering.

Abkhazia won the tournament on penalties, on home soil. President Raul Khajimba got on the microphone, as fans drove around blasting their horns and flying flags into the early morning, to declare the following day a national holiday.

* * * *

One of the better-known de facto states in CONIFA (with the proviso that yes, that is incredibly relative), Abkhazia is bordered to the south-east by Georgia, to the north by Russia and to the west by, erm, the Black Sea. Internationally recognised as part of Georgia by all but a small handful of nations, Abkhazia has been functioning as a separate state since the late 1990s, after a period of intense fighting between Abkhazian and Georgian forces.

Georgian troops entered the Abkhazian capital Sukhumi on 14 August 1992 in response to a declaration of independence. What followed was over a year of war, reminders of which are still littered throughout Sukhumi to this day.

One of the biggest structures in the city, the huge, brutalist 12-floor parliament building, was burned inside out in an intense period of shelling during the war. It has never been restored or revitalised, and remains as a silent monument to the conflict – the crumbling inside of the structure still accessible to the public.

Looking back through reports from the war, it's hard to see a 'right side' and a 'wrong side'. That happens a lot – people fighting for their lives in support or opposition of causes which mean something, or nothing. Both sides carried out atrocities. Both Georgian and Abkhaz forces were accused of wide-scale ethnic cleansing.

Not for the first or last time in a post-Soviet region, Russian involvement on the side of the separatists had been heavily implied, a Human Rights Watch report stating, 'The Russian role in this conflict has in part foreshadowed the brutal Russian behaviour in Chechnya, and has contributed to a pattern of Russian disregard for human rights and violations of the laws of war.'

While the British government still advises against all travel to Abkhazia, the situation has been relatively calm for over a decade now. A ceasefire is in effect, and five UN nations (Russia, Nicaragua, Venezuela, Nauru and Syria) formally recognise its self-declared statehood. That's more than many, but ... well, there's a hell of a lot more than five nations kicking around this planet.

Talking about Abkhazia in the context of the Abkhaz-Georgian war is necessary, but feels a bit old hat. What isn't mentioned about Abkhazia quite as much is that it's just staggeringly, eye-poppingly gorgeous.

There's a reason that Joseph Stalin had about half a dozen holiday homes scattered throughout the region. Take a second to put this book down (I know, you're close to the end, but I promise it'll still be there when you pick it back up) and search 'Lake Ritsa' in your search engine of choice (Google if you're normal; something that isn't Google if you're a monster).

The expanses of giant fir trees, the otherworldly deep blue of the water that simultaneously invites you in and looks alien, something too perfect, to be wary of, promising something beguiling in its depths. It's no surprise that there are multiple folk stories surrounding the lake; although the truth of what the blue depths are hiding is a little less romantic. It's mostly trout.

Abkhazia remains a place slightly out of time, with a lack of international recognition stalling what could be a booming tourism economy (seriously, look at that scenery, the routes up into the Caucasus Mountains, the ... just look at it!).

They've hosted two international sporting events, though. In addition to the CONIFA World Football Cup in 2016, there was the World Dominos Championship in 2011; 277 people entered. The USA's team had 18 members. Please don't ask me to explain any of that any further; it is all utterly absurd to me.

But yes. Football. Having beaten Panjab in the final in 2016 to spark wild celebrations in Sukhumi, Abkhazia flew to London two years later as one of the standout favourites to defend their title. Their squad was bolstered by the presence of former Russia Under-21 international Anri Khagush, a senior member of the travelling team at 31 and a veteran of two Champions League campaigns with Belarusian top flight side BATE Borisov.

A solid, sensible right-back, Khagush's debut in Europe's biggest competition was something of a baptism of fire; going to Spain to face a Real Madrid side who had been crowned La Liga champions for the second successive season just months previous. Khagush lasted an hour before he was sent off. BATE lost 2-0.

He was also sent off in his second Champions League campaign, six years later, in his second spell as a BATE player. Something about history running in cycles there, probably.

Occasional hot-headedness aside, though, Khagush has been a mainstay of a number of eastern European sides' defences throughout his career. His Abkhazia squad was augmented with a handful of players from the Russian league system and yet more who play in their home 'country', and looked … well, good. Solid.

A professional 3-0 win over Tibet kicked things off nicely, putting them top of the group after Northern Cyprus and Karpatalja drew in the following match at the Queen Elizabeth II Stadium – something that would be repeated much later in the competition.

And then, problems. Karpatalja pulled off a shock win over the reigning champions two days later, leaving Abkhazia needing to beat Northern Cyprus in their final group match to qualify for the quarter-finals, or face the indignity of being knocked out in the group stage of the tournament they were one of the favourites to win. The tournament that was meant to see them defend their title.

They drew 2-2 with Northern Cyprus. They got knocked out. From start to finish, it took four days and five hours for a title defence to start, stutter and end.

They dominated the placement rounds, of course – winning their three games by an aggregate score of 10-0 to finish as best of the rest, a 2-0 win over Kabylia putting an exclamation point on their campaign.

No parade this time, though. No national holiday for ninth place.

CONIFA's Hidden Rivalry

One of football's greatest delights is the relationships and friendships it can generate. Some fans make trips of thousands of miles every year to see a team they have no inherent connection to, and teams are twinned up with partners on the other side of the world on the basis of shared beliefs and a love of the game.

Sometimes the opposite happens.

Sometimes you get rivalries like the one between Brighton and Crystal Palace, now being played out in the top tier of English football. There's no reason for that rivalry to exist when it comes to proximity or political leanings, but that hasn't made it any less bitter since it all kicked off in the mid-1970s.

An FA Cup tie went on a little long – going to a third match, in the days before regular penalty shoot-outs et al. Young Brighton manager Alan Mullery threw a handful of loose change down in front of the Palace fans, shouted 'You're not worth that, Palace,' and was hustled away down the tunnel by police.

He claims that he'd had a cup of hot coffee thrown at him by one of the fans he insulted, but the reason didn't matter by that point. The A23 Derby (the road linking Brighton and Croydon, where Palace play) became a bona fide Thing.

Brighton fans knocked off Palace's nickname, fans got shouty and – ahead of a crucial play-off match in 2012, with a place in the Premier League up for grabs – somebody from the south coast side had done ... what's the polite way to say this? Done a big poo in the Palace dressing room. On the floor.

Football is full of these little battles, springing from a single match or moment. In England, Football League sides Swindon Town and Gillingham have a rivalry spanning 40 years after two games within a few weeks of each other, which saw multiple red cards, a fan knocking out the referee and a punch-up between players in the tunnel that landed two of them in court and one coach in hospital.

The phenomenon isn't just limited to domestic football, either. The USA and Ghana have developed an intense rivalry over the course of the 21st century, just by virtue of being drawn to play each other over and over again in crucial matches.

The pair met in three consecutive World Cups between 2006 and 2014, and each of their matches ultimately resulted in the other's elimination, a controversial penalty giving Ghana the win in 2006 before the African side proved the Americans' undoing four years later in South Africa, in a match that went all the way to extra time.

By the time the USA got their revenge in an absolutely barnstorming 2-1 win in 2014, there was an edge to the game. *This* was the one people were looking forward to. This was a chance for revenge, or a chance to keep up a winning record. Every tackle crunched just that little bit more.

American players deny that there's a real 'rivalry' there, but the American sports community barely understands a narrative that hasn't been carefully and deliberately constructed by TV stations.

For the Ghanaians' part, striker Kwesi Appiah said before a 'friendly' match between the two nations in 2017, 'There is clearly a rivalry developing between us and them because of the games that have been played at World Cup level. They have always been tough games with so much at stake, which has naturally always increased the intensity.'

Assistant coach Stephen Appiah, scorer of the controversial penalty which eliminated the USA from the World Cup a decade earlier, added, 'It will be easy to say this is just a friendly game but there is recent history between us so it won't simply be just a friendly game.'

What all of this is driving towards, of course, is that CONIFA has one of these rivalries, too. Of course it does. You get a bunch of football teams together, eventually two of them are going to start kicking lumps out of each other.

CONIFA isn't immune from that just because of a general message of inclusiveness. And so, to Western Armenia's feud with Panjab, which kicked off next to the Black Sea in 2016 and carried over to London two years later.

The 2016 tournament in Abkhazia was both sides' first entries into the World Football Cup and, after scoring 18 goals between them in their four group games, both reached the quarter-finals hopeful of securing a place in the last four.

Amar Purewal, named Asian Non-League Footballer of the Year in 2017, scored his second hat-trick in two games to smash Panjab into a 3-0 lead at half-time, Tamaz Avolian and Raffi Kaya hitting back in a hard-fought second half to bring Western Armenia right back into it and set up a grandstand finish.

The game finished 3-2, with both players and coaches clashing at the final whistle, on the pitch and in the tunnel.

When the two sides faced off in Slough two years later, it became obvious pretty quickly that some grudges were being held. The stands were packed with Panjab fans from the local community, creating the kind of partisan atmosphere rarely seen in CONIFA matches. To all intents and purposes, it was a home game for a Panjab side who are based in the UK, with all but two of their players British-born.

Charismatic Panjab FA president Harpreet Singh admitted to some hopes before the tournament that all of his side's group games being played at the same stadium in Slough would bring the local Panjabi community out in support, and he was vindicated. When Western Armenia's David Hovsepyan swung a dangerous elbow into Jhai Dhillon's face inside the opening minute of the match, he was met with a wall of boos and heckles from the main stand.

After a chat between referee and linesman, Hovsepyan was shown just a yellow card for the clear sending-off offence – the referee possibly mindful of 'spoiling' the match by creating a numerical mismatch for 89 minutes – and then the chaos began.

Vahagn Militosyan put the 'visitors' ahead after just 15 minutes, and made a point of riling the crowd up further, veering away to celebrate in front of the grandstand before taunting the fans and kissing the Western Armenia badge to a chorus of boos.

The game continued to be punctuated by tackles which stretched the point of legality, and Dhillon seemed a particular target for violence on the touchline, taking another swinging arm to the face from Militosyan in the first half only for no punishment to be handed out by the referee.

It's fashionable to blame the referees for matches where the actions of the players get out of hand … so I will. The fact that nobody was sent off for a full 90 minutes of the single dirtiest, angriest football match I have seen in my life still baffles me. Players flew into reckless, dangerous tackles knowing that their actions wouldn't have consequences (apart from for the person on the receiving end), teams surrounded the officiating staff to pressure them into decisions and, even though nine bookings were handed out over the 90 minutes, it could've been double that.

It feels a little cheap to reduce the Western Armenia team to a crude cliché of the team representing a people who have had to struggle, who themselves struggle against anyone and everyone – but their team plays with a chip on its shoulder.

From the off, they threw themselves at their opponents. Literally. The referee's whistle provided a constant soundtrack for the rest of the game.

A couple of Armenians, Hiraç Yagan particularly, indulged in the kind of high-level shithousery that Sergio Ramos would've been proud of. Two-footed tackles flew in, muscles were flexed, tempers flared. Militosyan's goal celebration told the story, sprinting halfway down the touchline tugging at his badge before being joined in a mass embrace by his team-mates and coaches.

The match ended in yet further tunnel confrontations, in shouting, and ultimately in both teams going through (the match finished at 1-0, which almost felt irrelevant in the aftermath).

Neither side made it out the other side of their quarter-final ties, Panjab losing 2-0 to Padania and Western Armenia being put to the sword by a Székely Land team who trounced them 4-0.

Expect to see some iron shin pads and maybe a protective box or two if both teams qualify for Somaliland 2020. You can't be too careful.

CONIFA World Football Cup 2018 Results

Group A:
Ellan Vannin 4-1 Cascadia
(Whitley 15', Jones 41', Caine 62', McVey 70' - Doughty 18')

Barawa 4-0 Tamil Eelam
(Sambou 17', Lucien 30' [pen], 80' [pen], Crichlow 43')

Barawa 1-2 Cascadia
(Bettamer 9' - Doughty 35', Morales 45')

Ellan Vannin 2-0 Tamil Eelam
(Whitley 47', Caine 57')

Barawa 2-0 Ellan Vannin
(Bettamer 40', Ismail 56')

Tamil Eelam 0-6 Cascadia
(Nouble 10' [pen], 87', Hayden-Smith 32', 71', Farkas 69', Ferguson 89')

Cascadia and Barawa progress

Group B:
Abkhazia 3-0 Tibet
(Akhvlediani 12', Maskayev 61', Shoniya 77')

Northern Cyprus 1-1 Karpatalja
(Mehmet 13' - I. Sandor 53')

Abkhazia 0-2 Karpatalja
(Gajdos 11', I. Sandor 90')

Northern Cyprus 3-1 Tibet
(Turan 2', 67', Gok 73' - Topgyal 38')

Abkhazia 2-2 Northern Cyprus
(Maskayev 21', Argun 90' [pen] - Kaya 27', Oshan 77')

Karpatalja 5-1 Tibet
(Gajdos 2', G. Sandor 36' [pen], Takács 42', 77', Svedjuk 75' - Yougyal 69')

Karpatalja and Northern Cyprus advance

Group C:
Székely Land 4-0 Tuvalu
(Bajko 23', 63', 68', Magyari 75')

Padania 6-1 Matabeleland
(Innocenti 10', 45', Piantoni 39', 42', Rosset 60', Rota 61' - Ndlela 78')

Székely Land 5-0 Matabeleland
(Fülöp 31' [pen], Gyorgyi 40', Magyari 42', 54', Hodgyai 90')

Padania 8-0 Tuvalu
(Corno 8', 12', 38', Ravasi 17', Valente 32', 44', 89', Rosset 71')

Padania 3-1 Székely Land
(Rolandone 19', Innocenti 27', Pllumbaj 45' - Szocs 90')

Tuvalu 1-3 Matabeleland
(Timuani 27' - S. Ndlovu 25', 38', Mlalazi 90' [pen])

Padania and Székely Land advance

Group D:
United Koreans in Japan 0-0 Western Armenia

Panjab 8-0 Kabylia
(Sandhu 24', 53', Purewal 45', 62', G. Singh 51' [pen], 90', K. Singh 75', 82')

United Koreans in Japan 0-0 Kabylia

Panjab 0-1 Western Armenia
(Militosyan 14')

Panjab 1-1 United Koreans in Japan
(Purewal 77' [pen] - Mun 90')

Western Armenia 4-0 Kabylia
(Mosoyan 23', Valenza-Berberian 61', 87', Militosyan 89')
Western Armenia and Panjab advance

Quarter-finals:
Barawa 0-8 Northern Cyprus
(Gok 15', 80', Onet 51', Turan 54', 69', Ali 58' [o.g.], Mehmet 84', Osman 88')
Padania 2-0 Panjab
(Innocenti 59' [pen], Pavan 90')
Karpatalja 3-1 Cascadia
(Gyürki 49', Takács 59', Gadjos 87' [pen] - Haddadi 80')
Western Armenia 0-4 Székely Land
(Tanko 36', Csizmadia 61', L. Fülöp 65', Bajko 86')

Semi-finals:
Northern Cyprus 3-2 Padania
(Mehmet 36', 84', Turan 80' - Ravasi 30', Pavan 47')
Karpatalja 4-2 Székely Land
(Toma 36', 57', Gyürki 75' [pen], Peres 90' - Csizmadia 77', Bajko 79')

Final:
Northern Cyprus 0-0 Karpatalja (Karpatalja win 3-2 on penalties)

Third Place Play-off:
Padania 0-0 Székely Land (Padania win 5-4 on penalties)

Placement Round – 5th-8th:
Barawa 0-5 Panjab
(K. Singh 8', 65', 72', 90', Minhas 46')
Cascadia 4-0 Western Armenia
(Ferguson 24', 62', Oldham 54', Farkas 79')

Placement Match – 5th/6th:
Panjab 3-3 Cascadia (Panjab win 4-3 on penalties)
(Virk 18', Minhas 24', 34' - Morales 45', Ferguson 54', 60')

Placement Match – 7th/8th:
Barawa 0-7 Western Armenia
(N. Hovsepyan, D. Hovsepyan, Yedigaryan, Guzel, Varjabetyan, Militosyan, Mosoyan)

Placement Round – 9th-16th:
Ellan Vannin 0-3 Tibet (Match forfeited by Ellan Vannin, automatic win awarded)
Matabeleland 0-0 Kabylia (Kabylia win 4-3 on penalties)
Abkhazia 6-0 Tamil Eelam
(Akhvlediani 40', 71', Logua 63', Shoniya 74', 88', Tarba 83')
United Koreans in Japan 5-0 Tuvalu
(Taniyama 18', Lee 20', 58', Shin 23', Mun 83')

Placement Round – 9th-12th:
Tibet 1-8 Kabylia
(Topgyal 43' [pen] - Baudia 25', 74', 77', 87', Hadid 45', Mezaib 49', 51', Bouabbas 81')

Abkhazia 2-0 United Koreans in Japan
(Akhvlediani 38', Kogoniya 78')

Placement Match – 9th/10th:
Kabylia 0-2 Abkhazia
(Logua 29', Zhanaa 56')

Placement Match – 11th/12th:
Tibet 1-1 United Koreans in Japan (UKJ win 4-1 on penalties)
(Yougyal 20' - Gelek 84' [o.g.])

Placement Round – 13th-16th:
Ellan Vannin 0-3 Matabeleland (Match forfeited by Ellan Vannin, automatic win awarded)
Tamil Eelam 4-3 Tuvalu
(Ragavan 7', 86', 90, Perananthan 90' - Petoa 3', 73', Vailine 55')

Placement Match – 13th/14th:
Matabeleland 1-0 Tamil Eelam
(Ndlela 81')

Placement Match – 15th/16th
Ellan Vannin 0-3 Tuvalu (Match forfeited by Ellan Vannin, automatic win awarded)

Final Placements:
1st: Karpatalja
2nd: Northern Cyprus
3rd: Padania
4th: Székely Land
5th: Panjab
6th: Cascadia
7th: Western Armenia
8th: Barawa
9th: Abkhazia
10th: Kabylia
11th: United Koreans in Japan
12th: Tibet
13th: Matabeleland
14th: Tamil Eelam
15th: Tuvalu
N/A: Ellan Vannin

Golden Boot:
Kamaljit Singh (Panjab) – 6 goals